# THE AWAKENING OF INTELLIGENCE: TOWARD A NEW PSYCHOLOGY OF BEING

## EASTERN PSYCHOLOGIES IN THE DIRECTION OF NEW TRANSPERSONAL THEORIES

## DIEGO PIGNATELLI SPINAZZOLA

IUNIVERSE, INC.
NEW YORK   BLOOMINGTON

The Awakening of Intelligence: toward
a new Psychology of Being
Eastern psychologies in the direction
of new Transpersonal Theories

iUniverse books may be ordered through booksellers or by contacting:

iUniverse
1663 Liberty Drive
Bloomington, IN 47403
www.iuniverse.com
1-800-Authors (1-800-288-4677)

Because of the dynamic nature of the Internet, any Web addresses or links
contained in this book may have changed since publication and may no longer
be valid.

ISBN: 978-1-4502-3213-5 (sc)
ISBN: 978-1-4502-3214-2 (ebk)

Printed in the United States of America

iUniverse rev. date: 9/15/2010

# CONTENTS

# CONTENTS

*I wish to dedicate this book to generous and special friends and pioneers of transpersonal psychology:*

Stanislav Grof
Stanley Krippner
Jim Fadiman
Stuart Sovatsky
Jenny Wade
Jorge Ferrer
Jean Houston
and Rick Tarnas

Using poetic and psychological language, interwoven with metaphors, Diego Pignatelli reveals the originality and creativity of Spiritual Awakening by exploring the findings of comparative mysticism and some of the new groundbreaking theories which lie behind the transpersonal movement. As well as the researcher's use of an accurate, descriptive and scientific style, Pignatelli articulates his writing with a sophisticated poetic language, centred around a particular *creative mythology*.

The author takes his reader into the adventurous territories of Transpersonal Psychology, providing us with theories by C. G. Jung and other authors of promising new theories such as Stanislav Grof, Richard Tarnas, Heinrich Zimmer, David Bohm, Abraham Maslow, Ken Wilber, Alan Watts, Abhinavagupta and Jiddu Krishnamurti.

The result is an eclectic leap into the invisible. This work makes a deep authentic appeal to an archetype of meaning which offers itself up as a new "meaning" of a "unifying symbol" in a society which no longer seems to be made up of archetypal meaning but which is actually "dissociated" from it.

Using a creative and poetic modality, Diego Pignatelli explores myth, religion, science and spirituality—the "liminal" territories of modern psychology. He introduces us to Transpersonal Psychology, Grof's holotropic paradigm and perinatal dynamics, mythology, oriental and Indian psychology, as well as Jungian and depth psychology. Pignatelli also discusses the fields of parapsychology, shamanism, thanatology, Near Death Experiences (NDE), Out of Body Experiences (OBEs—

astral travels occur during non-ordinary states of consciousness and travels to parallel universes through the Star Gates or "portals" of other mythological dimensions). He also teaches us about Kundalini awakening, mandala cosmology, altered/nonordinary states of consciousness (NOSC), psychedelic therapy and the implications of the new emerging paradigm whose holonomic theory and multidimensional psyche are currently explored by modern consciousness research.

*"A hero as well as a mystic is given the task of warning mankind of the errors towards which he is moving, and returning him to the vision of the ancients. The hero encourages mankind to pay attention to how far away Western culture has strayed from ancient meaning and from the truth, mysteries and enigmas of life which mankind currently finds inexplicable and irresolvable. Therefore, by moving away from what is presently considered as a "primitive" perception, mankind has actually turned away from the solid basis of mystic reality. Instead, he accepts and embraces a virtual reality which is meaningless."*

—*Diegō Pignatelli*

# FOREWORD

Diego Pignatelli's *Awakening of Intelligence* is a riveting book that explores transpersonal phenomena from a perspective that is crucially needed in a world that has been ripped apart by ignorance, fanaticism, and the lack of intelligence. The book is divided into three sections that begin with a pragmatic and experiential introduction to the thoughts of Alan Watts, Chuang Tzu, and Jiddu Krishnamurti. Following this, Pignatelli introduces concepts from both quantum physics and science fiction. Once his readers have finished this innovative perspective, Pignatelli takes them on a ride of altered states of consciousness ranging from Wilber and Grof's *pre-trans* theoretical debate to poetic narratives that link mythology, philosophy, religion, mysticism, and science fiction with the world of Transpersonal Psychology—a topic usually ignored by mainstream scholars. The third section concludes with an overview of transpersonal psychology that is enriched with the interface between creativity, philosophy, Indic mythology, science fiction, religion, and cutting edge research from quantum physics, near-death experiences, "archetypes of meaning," and the search for a "unifying symbol" within the human dimension in a society that seems to have lost the purpose of archetypal meanings is explored, concluding that society has become dissociated from this deep, inner connection. The result is a synthesis of various fields that unifies the meaning of altered states of consciousness in a way that will intrigue and electrify the reader's intellect.

Stanley Krippner, Ph.D., Professor of Psychology
Saybrook University, San Francisco, California

# INTRODUCTION

According to Barlach, "The creative individual, the hero, must evoke images of the future that need to get out of the night in order to give the world a new and better face."

*The Awakening of Intelligence* is a book that introduces the transpersonal vision from a point of view that I hope will be considered creative. Introducing the revelations of the visionaries along with the pioneering work of psychologists, scholars and researchers, all representative of contemporary spiritual thought between East and West, I bring the reader towards a new spiritual highway that runs full circle, and covers every aspect of consciousness treated by thinkers as diverse as Krishnamurti, Chuang Tzu and Alan Watts, from Heinrich Zimmer to C. G. Jung and Stanislav Grof, and from Ken Wilber to David Bohm.

The book is divided into three sections. First, a more pragmatic, experiential and biographical part introduces the thought of Alan Watts, Chuang Tzu, and Jiddu Krishnamurti. A second section introduces the transpersonal vision with the aid of new theories and images borrowed from quantum physics and science fiction. The third and final section is the Appendix, in which I present an overview of Transpersonal Psychology enriched within new images that represent an interface between creativity, psychology, philosophy, religion, mysticism, Indic mythology and science fiction.

*The Awakening of Intelligence* represents my own Promethean Awakening. In the course of the book, I have attempted to unite elements of philosophy and Indian mythology with Transpersonal Psychology. I use terms and concepts borrowed from Hindu philosophy and quantum mysticism, as explained in Michael Talbot book *The Holographic Universe* in which he illustrates the concepts of Quantum Mechanics, Holographic theory, holodecks, and parallel universes. In that way I create a link between new physics, mythology, transpersonal psychology and science fiction.

The result is an introductory synthesis of certain subfields of Transpersonal Psychology. My research in Transpersonal studies is described throughout this book, as well as in the Appendix. I transpose systematic research in this field into an integrative approach similar to Talbot's, but I have also poetically introduced the concept of star gates and sacred geometry to provide a creative touch. The goal is to offer readers a usable poetic mythology (linking the creative interface between mythology, philosophy, religion, mysticism and science-fiction) for the field of Transpersonal Psychology, something typically omitted by mainstream scholars.

In The *Awakening of Intelligence*, I remind the reader of a real spiritual and psychological need, with the hopes of helping him/her to rediscover his/her true identity with Brahman/Atman – the divine consciousness. Through a series of significant symbols of planes, lights and images, I reveal an "archetype of meaning" – a modern mythologeme full of symbolic and mythological resonances in which mysticism represents a bridge to the sacred and subtle realms of experience and interior dimensions. By reconsidering these dimensions, the reader will recognize himself/ herself as the Hindu *Tat Tvam Asi* (You Are It). Apart from having esoteric psychologies as an objective, another goal is to help the reader recognize his/her real identity by reintegrating the individual into the universal scheme of things. This provides the scope and synthesis of my book. The result is an eclectic leap into the invisible. This book makes a deep authentic appeal to an "archetype of meaning" which offers itself as a new "meaning" of a "unifying symbol" in the human dimension in a society which no longer seems to be founded upon purpose and archetypal meaning but instead is actually "dissociated" from it. Another synthesis that appears in the Appendix is my personal interpretation of the *pre-trans* theoretical debate, and discussions between Ken Wilber and Stanislav Grof.

In the prologue to the first chapter, I introduce one of the greatest and most eclectic philosophical thinkers of the twentieth century, Alan Watts, whose intelligent voice has inspired artists and followers of the American counter-culture. The first section of the second chapter of my book is therefore dedicated to Alan Watts, Ken Wilber and Jiddu Krishnamurti (a great spiritual teacher). In the second chapter, I explore Eastern philosophy from a deeply symbolic and archetypal point of view by introducing Tantric and Shaivite thought, e.g., Somananda, Abhinavagupta and Ksemaraja of the monistic Tantra schools of the 9th -11th centuries. Next, I introduce the figure of Avatar as a disciple of the Invisible, and I elucidate Indian philosophy and Shaivism. This chapter ends with a poetic passage entitled "Numinous: The Altar of the Sacred" which addresses symbolic and mystical claims.

The third chapter is a combination of complex themes: ranging from Tantra to Bohm's mystical, quantum concept of implicate and explicate orders. Next, I offer a hidden, concealed and invisible meaning that includes other orders of existence perceived not only by the mystics, but also by psychotics and schizophrenics, who only glimpse sporadic flickers of them. Finally, I extend Bohm's theory of an implicate order to include the god Shiva's cosmic dance.

With "Cosmic Waters in the Cosmogonic Dimension," I briefly articulate and introduce Indian mythology and psychology. In the concluding chapter of the last section I describe the archetypal dimension and archetypes as seen by Eastern and Western psychology. I show the importance of C. G. Jung and Erich Neumann's contributions regarding the collective unconscious and psychic dissociation of the current period. I also introduce Henry Corbin's *mundus imaginalis,* and in a section I expand on the connections between science fiction, quantum mysticism and Indian philosophy. To adumbrate the treatment there: I use the concepts of *maithuna,* the sacred or marriage couple (*Hieros Gamos*), Trikona Shakti-bindu who, with a double triangle inside a hexagon (called yantra Shivaite), taken together with the primordial archetypal constellations, are representative of star gates.

The Star Gate principle is seemingly not much different from mythology. In Egypt and Mesopotamia numerous rites for accessing the threshold already expressed this numinous place which symbolised the Great Mother and dolmen. One door connects the passage from the female uterus to rebirth. The dolmen however, as Neumann maintained, is the "sacred house and its expansion is not only created by a temple but generally by a "sacred abode" (Neumann, Erich. 1972. *The Great Mother*. Princeton, NJ: Princeton).

I identify this expansion in the Star Gate: the dolmen which connects a region of space and time to another so that it represents a genuine wormhole. Star Gate is not only a fantastic metaphor, it is also the same symbolic and transpersonal gateway, through religions and myths, represents humanity.

The Appendix is dedicated to Transpersonal Psychology. Starting with Jung and Zimmer, I have tried to compare the Jungian symbolism of the mandala of quaternity with the Indianist Zimmer's Yantra (a two-dimensional mandala with four gates). This is synthesized into what is hopefully an original theory borrowing from science fiction: Star Gate, the door of fear, which is a sacred geometry providing a gateway to other parallel and invisible dimensions (Shiva Loka). These are dynamic wormholes which I identify with the *pancavaktra* or the five faces of the god Shiva, whose gate guardians (Dvrapalas, also known as guardians of four cardinal directions, or Lokapalas) are placed at the threshold of the Hindu temples.

These *pancavaktra* are dynamic archetypes, prisons of cosmic illusion in the samsara in the field of the normal state of consciousness, but they are also doors to the invisible in an illuminated condition. I also present the *pancavaktra* as energetic dynamics which have the capacity to move a particular karmic configuration. My discovery is that samsara and nirvana are a geometric karma or a two-sided coin which holds a human being in check. In the subsequent paragraph "Mandala: the Holographic Receptacle," I discuss Tantra and the Jungian theory of *Selbst* understood as a *rotundum* or mandala. Centering my argument on the mandala and on the process of identification with a pre-selected divinity (Idam-Ishtadevata), I indicate the process of the renewal of consciousness and the revulsion of plan, as described in the Shaivite tradition; I also indicate a similarity with the ancestor of modern psychology: exorcism.

Next I describe the kaleidoscopic, holographic dimension of reality, from the Buddhist point of view of the void (*sunyata*) and atomic theory or *dharma* (*svabhava / svadharma*). The paragraph contains various elements such as kaleidoscopic vision, the holographic paradigm, Buddhist logic or metaphysic and Star Gates, which I believe to be hidden thresholds in the universe. Here the ancestral, phylogenetic, karmic and mythological depository of humanity resides. After this, I give a brief presentation or introductory synthesis of the holotropic work of Stanislav Grof.

As I explore the dynamics of Stanislav Grof's perinatal psychology, I compare his work on systematic self-exploration of non ordinary states of consciousness on a fetal level in the regressive stage (named "back door" by Wilber) with Wilber's "front door" concept. My thesis favours Grof's work rather than Wilber's transpersonal-centaur model, which tends to be more reserved about the pre-ego level. I develop my point of view using Wilber's front door concept and transpersonal regression, moving towards Grof's proposed back door in the perinatal level of the unconscious. I take this to be a legitimate and authentic dimension of human experience and criticise Wilber's assumption that transpersonal levels are only at the service of the ego (ego transcendence) instead of already being present at a childlike pre-ego level as Grof believes.

The last two sections are based on wormholes or star gates whose dynamic of the psyche are the *pancavaktra*: the enclosure or the prisons of the mind which act as a two-sided coin glimpsed at the threshold of liberation. In the same paragraph I introduce psychological terms such as psychic, metapsychic and trans-psychic in order to define the *samadhi*/wormholes of meditative absorption in the three states of consciousness following by a fourth state (*turiya*). This state was recognised by the seers of Rig Veda, who opened themselves up to the wormholes or star gates of parallel worlds and entered into the sublime domain of Shiva, Vishnu and Brahma paradise, practising *Vira-sadhana* in adoration of the great goddess Mother Kali.

I attribute a special section to Stanislav Grof and his revolutionary discovery with LSD in the new uncharted territories of consciousness in the then-new area of Transpersonal Psychology. Grof proposes an unexplored journey into new dimensions of the psyche and of the unconscious. In the paragraph dedicated to Grof, I have compared his experiential model of the basic perinatal matrices (BPMs) to virtual holographic simulations made up of holodeck, borrowed from the popular television series "Star Trek: The Next Generation."

With my synthesis of the kundalini syndrome and its corresponding symptoms (see Lukoff, Lu, Turner, DSM-IV Association for Humanistic Psychology: 1998), I stress the importance of Jung's discoveries of the last century. These were discoveries which were based on the psychological significance of the mandala.

Finally, I conclude this review with a synthesis of Grof's and Wilber's work and discuss the pre-trans fallacy and Wilber's fascinating spectrum model, in addition to his omission of perinatal dynamics as he refers only to the post-natal model. Grof's model of the psyche I include in contrast because it is broader, more transpersonal and trans-biographical.

The key to reading the *Awakening of Intelligence* is metaphor. A creative metaphor interweaves image, poetry, myth and spirituality. The mythologeme is a language that is expressed for images and is charged with mythical image "nouveau enriched" from potentiality of meaning. No language can reach the expressive riches of the mythical image. On the contrary of the mythologeme that is an original language and that it is expressed by metaphors. Every word/symbol/image in the context of the *Awakening of Intelligence* is a metaphor. It is fantastic metaphor that in the Star Gate sees the encounter between mythology and science fiction; a paradoxical one in Chuang Tzu, in which the holy uses the metaphor of the paradox to scorn human madness; and a metaphor expressing the anti-conventional and the "not sense" in Alan Watts. The metaphor becomes experiential, connecting the holodeck (virtual holographic simulation or holographic room where everything happens) with the theoretical paradigm of the basic perinatal matrices. The latter concept in particular was used in the context of the systematic self-exploration in the holotropic research of Stanislav Grof.

The myth is metaphor that reflects the philosophy of ancient India in connection with the groundbreaking discoveries of the astrophysics and of the quantum physics that rediscover and interpret the dance of Shiva to explore the mystery of the universe and of the dynamics of the wormholes.

In the unfolding process of its poetic language, the *Awakening of Intelligence* is enriched of a new aesthetic sensibility interpreting an academic literature, that of transpersonal, and uplifting it to a more creative level. In that manner, I try to interpret studies of systematic and scientific researches poetically, enriching them with a new tone and a new light. The result is a creative interface between mythology, psychology, mysticism, quantum physics, astrophysics and science fiction.

My book offers what I hope will be seen as insights, and proposes them as a novel compendium, reflecting a broad range of literature around the subject, including authors such as Michael Talbot, Stanislav Grof, C. G. Jung, Bohm, Krishnamurti, Abhinavagupta, William James, Alan Watts and Ken Wilber.

By producing an elaborate synthesis of the most important trends in transpersonal and spiritual studies, I hope that *The Awakening of Intelligence* can be a motivational and creative tool for future generations of scholars, as well as a bridge which spans creative bases for spiritual and mystical levels, opening up new avenues for interpreting and exploring transpersonal phenomena.

# PRAISE

Diego Pignatelli is a gifted visionary and writer with encyclopedic understanding of spiritual psychologies whose book uplifts the reader toward the very mystical states that all the great saints have described.
—**Stuart Sovatsky, PhD,** Author of *Words From the Soul* and *Your Perfect Lips*

*The Awakening of Intelligence* is a remarkable book. Diego Pignatelli has presented an original and provocative perspective on this topic, a perspective that is crucially needed in a world that has been ripped apart by ignorance, fanaticism, and the lack of intelligence.
—**Stanley Krippner, PhD**, Professor of Psychology, Saybrook Graduate School, San Francisco, California

*The Awakening of Intelligence* is a wonderful compendium of contemporary transpersonal thought. Pignatelli has produced a very necessary synthesis of the most important trends in transpersonal scholarship and spiritual studies.
—**Jorge N. Ferrer**, Author of *Revisioning Transpersonal Theory: A Partecipatory Vision of Human Spirituality*

Diego Pignatelli's metaphor of the holodeck very intriguing as a way to envision the kinds of altered-state material that arises during holotropic breathwork. It seems like a good, contemporary explanation for what were previously called the "imaginal worlds" of altered states, since many seem to have similar imagery and "rules of operation." I think Pignatelli's construct is an intriguing metaphor that opens up new avenues of explanation and exploration for nonordinary phenomena.
—**Jenny Wade, PhD,** Author of *Changes of Mind: A Holonomic Theory of Evolution of Consciousness*

# PREFACE

*The Awakening of Intelligence* aims to put meaning back into the archetype of the symbol, something which seems lost in this society. It is complex but rich in arguments, concepts and images which reflect not only the wide spectrum of transpersonal psychology but also threads interwoven with symbols.

States which C. G. Jung called "psychoid experiences" also perceive these symbols from a consciousness which looks at the divine to the synthesis of a mystic union. The struggle between good and evil, between children of the night and children of the day, is the emblem of the cosmogonic archetype which struggles in the shadows of consciousness. Finally, it opens up to the primordial and multi-dimensional splendour of the collective unconscious.

Its invisible realms are archetypes, stones, jewels, diamonds of a "numinous" treasure rejected *a priori* by humanity which does not want to give this, the gold of revelation, the shaman of the prophets in front of the city of the gods, any symbolic significance.

The cosmogonic dimension – rediscovery – is rejected by man who, admitting that reality is dead, has relegated the gods to their paradise, where they become pathologies that torment consciousness like children of the Night, with a fluid and rebellious archetype which escapes man's and destiny's control.

Symbolically enriched with different tones, this book aims to appeal to the Invisible, to Intelligence as well to the Myth and the discoveries of Stanislav Grof, Ken Wilber, Joseph Campbell, David Bohm, Stanley Krippner, Stuart Sovatsky and other transpersonal theorists.

The sacredness of being seems like "an alchemy of symbols, the game of two lovers who betray each other and then regain unity once more in a mystic wedding celebration" which finally it opens the way for man, in his escape from the gods, to rediscover of a hidden meaning. The invisible interface between these two states acts as a parallel reality, vision and prophecy.

It is from this "cosmic game" revealed in a symbolic alchemy, that the book leads to an extraordinary Reawakening of Shiva from the Invisible which shapes our perceptions into a phenomenal seat of illusion. This is because the gods have turned pale and have hidden their symbols far away from human mediocrity, far away from a world which has already chosen how things should be by following the path of lying. *The Awakening of Intelligence* breaks this lie by making contact with spiritual realities and their laws, which do not belong to this order of existence but an underlying existence, similar to the American physicist David Bohm's implicate order. From the order laws appear to be invisible, a three-dimensional tapestry, a hologram, in which the symbol reflects its projection.

Hidden worlds interact in the fabric of life and our perceptions. It is Shiva's reality, it is his dance which pulses in the metaphysical universe in which Hindus projected their visions.

Now we are far away from those realities, but transpersonal studies reflect those visions propelling them again into a new revolutionary pattern which is overtaking the Newtonian-Cartesian paradigm in a new vision of the Cosmos.

Parallel studies like those of Stanislav Grof, Richard Tarnas, Fritjof Capra, Fred Alan Wolf, Jorge Ferrer and Ken Wilber have advanced extremely modern theories which, having thrown academic science (still based on the classic Newtonian-Cartesian model) into discussion, are revaluating and reshaping other theories accessible to both the scientist and the mystic. From here, from the great effort to reconcile science with religion and reconvert the pragmatism of the West to the sacred mysticism of the East, attempts have been made, but they have never opened up to extraordinary and non-ordinary external reality.

Transpersonal Psychology is an advocate of this reality, opening up the way to the mystic and scientist just as to an artist with such privileges.

Access to what is sacred and invisible is an accessible and at the same time inaccessible reality. We need to distinguish this numinous quality described by C. G. Jung and see it as a whole in the cosmic tapestry of consciousness, in this cosmic hologram which is close to the vision of our predecessors, prophets and mystics of all the ages.

# ACKNOWLEDGMENTS

My greatest joy is to have the opportunity to thank all the exceptional beings who generously offered me the time, support and friendship.

I owe thanks above all to Stanley Krippner, who generously offered me his time and friendship throughout our correspondence, and before the completion of this book. I owe him a great debt of gratitude for being an extraordinary friend and teacher.

I want also to thank Stuart Sovatsky for his great presence in my life and for being a friend and companion on this spiritual journey.

Their enthusiastic encouragement, support and expecially loving presence have enriched my Hero's journey.

I owe special gratitude to Marcie Boucouvalas and all the JTP staff, and above all to

Stanislav Grof, whose original work, insights and brilliant genius have inspired and stimulated me throughout my experiential inner journey in holotropic states. He has had a great influence on own understanding

*Diego Pignatelli Spinazzola*

of the transpersonal vision and sense of the "visionary insight for nonordinary states of consciousness." The potentiality of the integrative purpose and meaning of Stanislav Grof's work has been of fundamental importance in my life.

I want also thank Jorge Ferrer, for paving me the way to the transpersonal field and to Rick Tarnas for being a true friend and teacher.

I want to thank Jim Fadiman, for his generousity and friendship, and Jenny Wade for the interesting exchange about transpersonal matters. A special thank to Kathleen Erickson, Joyce Kovelman and Jean Houston who greatly appreciated the mythopoetic prose of my work.

Finally I want to thank Caroline Swettenham and Adam Kay for their precious help with the translation and the editing of the current edition of this book.

I cannot conclude this acknowledgement without including my own family, my mother Celeste and my brother Luca, who shares with me many of the spiritual and of philosophical interests throughout my ongoing journey.

# II Foreword

## Awakening of Intelligence: A Psychology of the Sacred

*The Awakening of Intelligence* is enriched *via* tones and images, parables, and mythological fairytales that introduce the reader to transpersonal psychology and its spiritual dimensions. The doorway and final scope of this endeavour is to bring together ancient religious systems and Eastern traditions with contemporary symbols and the science of Transpersonal Psychology, a bridge with the Sacred as in the famous keywords *Tat Tvam Asi*: You Are It. The scope of this book is to bring together the sacred marriage (*Hieros Gamos*) between mythos and logos—between cosmos and psyche, and between the spiritual creative inspiration of the Mythos and the collective unconscious of the Psyche.

Jenny Wade a Ph.D professor at Pacifica Graduate School and University of Santa Barbara,once reading my work said "his metaphor of the holodeck (presented below in the book) is very intriguing as a way to envision the kinds of altered-state material that arises during holotropic breathwork. It seems like a good, contemporary explanation for what were previously called the 'imaginal worlds' of altered states, since many seem to have similar imagery and 'rules of operation'" and she added that it is "an intriguing metaphor that opens up new avenues of explanation and exploration for nonordinary phenomena."

These metaphors would represent contemporary imaginal worlds (*mundus imaginalis*) that are found in science fiction, in Stanislav Grof's holotropic and experiential framework, and in Jung's collective unconscious. The poetic forms and metaphors represent the greatest strengths in this context, and are also creative expressive tools for a Transpersonal Psychology described here.

I offer a new interpretation of the Shaivite's *tantras* and *agamas,* as well as many of Jung's concepts and the emerging paradigm of quantum physicists (see Bohm's implicate order and the ancient *Rig Veda*). The Appendix serves as a tribute to transpersonal psychology by introducing new modern father figures such as Stanislav Grof, Ken Wilber, and David Bohm along with their profoundly significant theories. In this regard, I also introduce Wilber's concept of pre-trans fallacy, and discuss Grof's perinatal matrices and theories that question some of the concepts espoused by mainstream psychology. The transpersonal dimension of "individuation process," or Jung's *Selbst*, is possible only through the reactivation of specific archetypes in the modern psyche, along with their projecting symbols. By reactivating these archetypes and symbols in both the individual and the collective consciousness, a new Intelligence is awakened and blends with the newest symbols of transpersonal psychology to create a science of the sacred.

# II PREFACE

*The Awakening of Intelligence* is also Shiva's Reawakening.
It is the symbol of light, desire, willingness and creativity.
Shiva is the Creative Consciousness—something which
is perfectly understood by Shiva, the supreme hero of
gods, the master of the universe. He destroys and reorders
the Cosmos. The divine consciousness has reawakened.
Shaivism is a mystical, esoteric knowledge which elevates
consciousness to super-consciousness.

In the course of my studies I have concentrated on
other more "alternative" disciplines which integrate the
same *tantra*. The theory of transpersonal psychology is one
of my interests, as it draws on Hindu and Buddhist mystics
and Sufism – a real psychology of sacredness, which Jung
anticipated in his study of archetypes and its myths. These
are myths which take you back to the beginnings and re-
examine "mystic states of a consciousness which looked at
the divine and saw the subtle worlds sewn together with
sacred material where cosmogonic heroes fight against
terrible demons who are the children of the Cosmic
Night." The rishi of India unveil this philosophical matrix

through Veda, the context of a cosmogonic dimension in which the entry point, through trans-conscious states, was sacred. Yogis opened the way to domains which were not of their current world, uncovering in a clairvoyant state a trans-dual experience. They could enter the sacred realms of Shiva, Indra, Vishnu or Agni and adore the ferocious Kali by practising *vira-sadhana*, the untamed beasts of the Goddess of Time.

These same mystics of the Orient were capable of opening the Sacred Ancestral Doors: dimensions not wholly theirs, but synchronised in parallel with their intuitive perceptions. This is how the yogi entered into the trans-dual domain of Absolute Truth. They entered the sublime paradise of Shiva, the seats of the cult (*kula*) of the god and his consort Shakti, the revealing mouth of the divine. They gave offerings to the idols in the sanctuaries and in the stupa made by microcosmic projections reflected in the Hindu macrocosm. We are not surprised to find that the World Axis par excellence the *kailasanatha* (reproductions of Kailasha the sacred house of Shiva in the complex of Ellora) called back to the sacred Hindu Mountain of Meru, the cosmic centre from which the Axis Mundi is linked to the entire universe.

In my interpretation of Abhinavagupta I have discussed some pieces which, apart from *tantra*, are the driving force of the book. Drawing from the work of Alan Watts, the marvellous interpreter of Zen and Buddhism, Jiddu Krishnamurti (in my version "the intelligence of compassion"), as well as Chuang Tzu, there emerges a key post-modern re-reading to the modern theories of holograms. Thus some of the key universal holons revisited by Transpersonal Psychology have managed to find a coherent metaphysical synthesis where the spiritual is joined with super-mental – the Atman is joined with the Brahman.

Transpersonal Psychology is the fulcrum of theories which so often surpass the aesthetic, the academic and disciplinary fields. It is the modern day mystic. The key to reading the book is the spiritual metaphor, as well as the mystic union in which the self re-appropriates itself in its cosmogonic dimension. In the general rejection and elimination of a collective madness, numinosisty, to use one of Jung's terms, appears iridescent and irrelevant in the eyes of humanity. The symbolic gold of the sacred revelations is rejected a priori by a humanity interested in dead and false stereotypes and "false myths." "Life is a parable, an 'alchemy of symbols' which, like a young couple, betray each other and then reunite in mystic wedding nuptials."

In the chapter "The Cosmogonic Mandala: The Escape from the Gods," I introduce the mandala as primitive man's urgent metaphysical and meta-psychic need. As a supernatural projection of a hetero-spatial extension and like a game of cosmic involution in which our era is enveloped and regresses as if in a Samsaric vortex, the *trimurti* watch over the game of the universe. This is the point.

In "Tantra, the Mystic of the Universe," I present the phonemic and knowledgeable iter according to Ksemaraja. The last section of the book is dedicated to the discovery of holograms which are reality in three-dimensional forms or as in the case of *yantra*, two-dimensional forms. "A hologram can enclose a mandala, since what the hologram has in common with the mandala is universal projected

*Diego Pignatelli Spinazzola*

reality." Stanislav Grof, Ken Wilber, Abraham Maslow, C. G. Jung and William James provide the unifying knowledge of these dimensions which are hidden behind the trans-psychic door of the universe (Star Gate, the portal).

In the book I have used cosmogonic Hindu parables such as the episode of the liberation of cosmic water by Indra evoked by the rishi, the seers of this prehistoric mystic celebrated in the Vedas. In this era we are rediscovering spirituality through the Myth which has always taught that there is a sacred door hidden behind the universe. A return to mysticism is a meta-symbolic way of reaching what is divine once more.

# II INTRODUCTION

We are in an age of Darkness. In this dual, elusive and difficult fight, there is an archetype which made the gods flee from Mount Olympus: the archetype of the Word.

Theological and metaphysical speculations have deposed mysticism, which is, more than knowledge itself, a conscience of the godly, a place where the divine itself finds the voice.

Man has barricaded himself behind ideology and a dogmatic faith in conventions and its useless adjuncts. Man has snubbed the care of the gods.

There isn't a place for the Tao here, "the celestial model" sent forth from the ancient ones.

In this deviancy man could not but surrender to a meek participation, an alienation, to a collective escape from the sacred.

In the conventional act the laws of man have taken the place of the "divine laws" and its archetypes (archetypon).

If the Sanskrit root of the word "div" is "to access," we may also affirm that the entrance to this access is closed to a human consciousness that identifies with modern ideologies, in the theological, philosophical speculations and metaphysical disquisitions which frame human ignorance (avidya).

In the preceding century, revolutionary changes have taken place. Men such as Alan Watts who have explained, in an eclectic and post-modern language, the simple nature of the Tao, the philosophy of the ancients.

What Watts tried to achieve was to free the Tao from the crusting of modern philosophy, that came from the Aristotle's metaphysics and a mechanistic vision of the world.

What we may see in Watts is the image of a precursor.

The Tao, the way, like water, is fluid and easy to shape and may not be captured by the speculative nature of human beings and become their subject.

To follow the nature of the *wei wu wei* (literally: action without action) means reapproaching the divine in a passive and neutral mode, where every dualistic division between subject and object sheds its boundaries, called back to the primordial One of the Hindu Vedanta religions.

All is illusion for the *jivan mukta* (the liberated in life) who contemplates the cosmic game and partakes to it. All being partakes in the magnificent dance of Shiva.

That is why this century has been dominated by many attempts to reach the sacred, similar to the attempt to reach a complete command over all, but very few realizations have happened on the higher planes.

Maya, the cosmic illusion as manifestation of game (in Sanskrit: *lila*), has always woven the thread in human evolution. We are victims of a pathology that sees in the human emancipation a conscious escape from the sacred.

This conscious or human hyper-consciousness is the punishment of the gods. The punishment for having fled the skies, choosing the way of action, as the Taoists used to say, with the well-known words of Chuang Tzu.

The being is called to a new awareness. In Krishnamurti, all this finds its place in the choiceless awareness, where the actual deliverance is the one to be attained from the sheath of psychological time. Krishnamurti shall be a constant reference point also for the new trans-humanistic transpersonal psychology which will, from Abraham Maslow onward, spread in several fields of research, aiming to study mysticism by finding a common denominator between philosophies, sciences and the Eastern religions.

I should add that the archetypal dimension is not only wished for by C. G. Jung as a remedy to the "human pathology of the Soul" but also as a higher stage, the one that Maslow will call "Peak Experience."

The study of the trans-personal brings a new light, opening new ways, ways which are not only akin to the modern science of sub-atoms and higher energies but also to the human necessity which is always of spiritual nature. If Ken Wilber, neo-exponent of the Integral Psychology, wishes for a diurnal Vision of the Kosmos and a revision of all conventional psychologies, we also wish that this spectrum, this holon of whole, will become our spiritual and diurnal vision of the Kosmos.

# III INTRODUCTION

This book represents not only an artistic and creative growth but an evolutional continuum in my research in Eastern philosophies.

With a open glance to the mystical approach of holistic doctrines such as Buddhism, Zen Buddhism and Vedanta, and in a sort of growing of themes, the book moves toward that spiritual highway shown by mystics of all the time: from Alan Watts to Jiddu Khrisnamurti to Chuang Tzu, up to the neo-founders of the Integral and Transpersonal Psychology, Ken Wilber and Stanislav Grof.

Extending the themes of such authors with a personal new elaboration of the argumentations, I set to take, to awaken the reader in the Great Field of Being, to the search of a new psychology.

The book offers several cornerstones. From the dialectic of Krishnamurti to the synthesis of his thought and teachings, to the exhortations of Alan Watts, ready to unsheathe Zen, like a surprising, sarcastic nonsense aiming to liberation as the result of a radical inversion of perspective. Such realization is supported by the Eastern philosophies that are not only given to a mystical yearning, but also to a pragmatic "doing." Zen meditation is active, such as the art of a fencer or a judoka who has to defend from sudden attacks coming from all sides. It is in the wondrous surprise the Alan Watts' art of Zen, right in the face of every religious dogmatism the *wei wu wei* (literally: not doing) is the remedy against all the evils of our conformist and homologated society. It is the *wei wu wei*, this unselfconscious flowing in the awareness of the Zen moment (*satori*), pillar and milestone of a wisdom that has in Lao Tzu the forefather and in Chuang Tzu the interpreter. It is the tradition of the *wei wu wei* that these great thinkers have in common, therein lies the antidote to social convention, that Procustean bed to which we all tend to adjust.

In the use of the paradox, *wei wu wei* becomes emblematic, setting in as an intuitive mode at the centre of the macrocosm, the *Axis Mundi* as seen by the Hindus: the Brahman.

In the quick deconstruction of fear, without reacting to it, is still the *wei wu wei*, as a passive mode that is found in Krishnamurti's choiceless awareness, the perception freed by the monotony of the becoming and the obsession of time and pain. "This becoming, this psychological time, is and interval and in this interval we suffer because we hang between what 'it is' and what it 'should be'." "The awareness of the existence of these two probabilities sees in the exhortation of Krishnamurti, the actual victory of "the being against the deceitful and utopical of the psychological becoming."

In the dynamics implied in the encounter between the becoming and the being I highlighted the iconoclastic pragmatism, the awakening of the spiritual intelligence of Krishnamurti, who is freed by every psychological scheme and therefore delivered from the structure of time.

From Krishnamurti comes the warning that will be a foreword to the new studies on awareness and transcendence. It will be the age of the transpersonal psychology, the fourth strength which emerged among the trans-humanistic currents of Abraham Maslow, aimed to the study of mysticism, trance, of the psychedelic experiences and above all to self-healing.

From transpersonal psychology, I bring forth in synthesis Ken Wilber's holonic meta-theories, a neo-exponent of an eclectic, syncretic thought between philosophy, physics, metaphysics and psychology.

In this context I place a study on the archetypes as seen by the Hindu cosmogony. I mentioned the name of a great explorer and father of this new generation of scientists of the psychology. I am talking about C. G. Jung, whose studies on archetypal models have opened a wide spectrum of directions for new research.

There is a strong signal which comes from the depth of these studies, which put together holistic theories of psycho-integrative methods of research to the great religions and philosophies of the Eastern traditions. The supply of these theories goes with the outcome of an iter of experiences, which is wealth of teachers, yogis and spiritual guides, is now freer as it ever was to the Great Ground of Being, of which, once again we are part of.

# CHAPTER I
# THE AWAKENING OF
# INTELLIGENCE

## Transpersonal – Ken Wilber's Flexible and Invisible Kosmos

Let us begin this temporary journey with Alan W. Watts, the man who more than any other has put forward key interpretive intuitions and has built a bridge in terms of oriental wisdom between the strange tendencies of the modern conventional world and oriental religions. This he has done using the simple language of imperceptible tones, touching on brilliant intuitions which have gone far beyond the common understanding of things. The eclecticism of Alan Watts remains and will continue to remain an example for all the "inner researchers" or "masters of life" who will look to his interpretations.

This is not the case with Ken Wilber. He is the promoter of new sciences in the transpersonal currents which have definitively eclipsed the old approaches of conventional psychology. He is indebted to authors of the calibre of Alan Watts. The paradigms which are being constructed open up a new vision of a sublimated reality with intuitions which go beyond matter and logic in order to move layers on a metaphysical and trans-mental level, and move towards a unifying awareness of the entire universe (Brahman). Consciousness opens up to new structures like holons "a whole which is part of other wholes" as defined by Wilber who, by using scientific research in the bio-physical field and with the help of oriental religions, has managed to continue the work of his predecessors. He opens a bridge to spiritual wisdom, which, more than any other science, is the divine source of existence.

Transpersonal psychology is the new driving force which is colliding with other fields, thanks to scientists like Ken Wilber, Stanislav Grof, Allan Combs, Richard Tarnas, Jorge Ferrer, Stuart Sovatsky, Roger Walsh, Marcie Boucouvalas, Frances Vaughan, James Fadiman, Stanley Krippner and other pioneers of the revolutionary, trans-humanistic counter-movement founded in the United States. Not only is it colliding with fields of research but social fields as well and, unlike psychology or psychiatry, it is moving towards the sensitivity of the subject, converting his/her psychological, existential or emotive unease which also gets defined as a pathological order into a radical self-healing and self-awakening. This attempt to sensitise vis-à-vis anxious subjects and the methodology of integration make transpersonal psychology the spokesperson (as a shamanic healer) for the innate potentialities in a human being.

So, sensitising to conventionally defined pathological or "borderline" types, transpersonal psychology considers a human being's own experience as not yet awakened, the "confines" between the conventional, empirical world and absolute reality, everything to compose a unique, indivisible whole defined by Vedanta as "The breath of the Universe."

The transpersonal current leans on this universal level, on this indivisible whole, inserting itself by right in the metaphysical and meta-psychic framework of things. On the transpersonal level we are neither psychotic nor depressed nor borderline. We are all children of Brahman. We do not realise that Brahman is dancing above us and that, like the dance of a molecule or electrons, Brahman has never stopped fascinating us. It is for this reason that researchers like Wilber, Tart and Engler – the main supports of transpersonal study – work hard in this amazing field of research, widening consciousness until it reaches the portals of the universe.

With the well-advanced discoveries of Perennial Philosophy, Wilber and his colleagues have come to describe the "Great Field of Being" as an organised universe where each level transcends the preceding one in a "holonic modality." A holon is a whole which is part of wholes, in this case referring to consciousness, we can say that one's level varies from matter-mental-spiritual to transpersonal and non-dual. Each level can integrate the preceding one and transcend it. Our universe is like a Kosmos with several waves and these tune in to ascertained levels. We can say that with Wilber each holon flows into the current of this invisible Kosmos.

The Kosmos is an organised, operating unit with "holonic representations." As is understood by Wilber, the basic waves of the Great Field of Being are the general levels across which numerous different lines and currents of development flow on an emotive level of realisation. Wilber's Kosmos is a "lattice work," an amalgamation of lots of currents along which the basic holon-waves flow and are predisposed. Holons are also definite structures in a holistic embrace. To use one of Wilber's cheerful metaphors—they are the waves which flow in the "Great River of Life."

The levels are equal to levels of existence, neighbouring the physical-sensorial-mental-spiritual-non-dual fulcrums. Such fulcrums do not have rigid borders so that one level, be it pre-personal (physical-emotive) or personal (rational) can transcend the last one and approach "subtle" levels in the Great Chain of Being, that is to say the spheres of super-consciousness. These dimensions open up to interconnected realms (Realms of Brahma) transcending common, dualistic perception and open up to the shining, experiential light of All-Brahman. Brahman is the holon-consciousness of Everything but if it is tied to illusory perception (maya) it is also its reflection (abhasa). Pathologies, which are nothing more than temporarily open or frozen potentials, are grafted from this "false perception."

The experience of opening up is at the apex of "transpersonal" levels, more precisely the psychic-subtle-causal level in the Great Ground of Being, culminating in the non-dual identification with Brahman. On the subtle and psychic level consciousness is intuitive and can have a basic or intermittent archetypal vision. It is through its successive opening up on the causal level, which even the archetypal base transcends, that one accesses the shapeless realms of non-duality.

These theories are the fruit of an experiential course, the heritage of centuries of masters, yogis and spiritual guides. Modern studies are proposing a scientific synthesis from which they use the main theorists like Ken Wilber, D. P. Brown and Stanislav Grof with their own cartographies of consciousness. More than any others they promote a theory with a holistic approach, where oriental philosophies are also assuming a role determined by subsequent discoveries.

# KRISHNAMURTI
# THE INTELLIGENCE OF
# COMPASSION

Across the '50s and the '60s and at the end of the '80s, Jiddu Krishnamurti, of Indian origins, moved around the world, in what was meant to be a new spiritual journey that brought him in a "land without paths." By many called a prophet, a messianic vehicle comparable to the new Maitreya, Krishnamurti will set with coherence the experiment both the leaving of his motherland India and the getting acquainted with the West. Away from that pain and poverty, which was a strong characteristic of his native village Madanapalle, he was placed under the tutorship of Anne Besant who was the main exponent of the Theosophical society, near Madras. The young Krishnamurti seemed a reckless lord, but that was not meant to be his destiny. Like the Buddha in his youth, he dwelt among the luxury of a royal palace which kept him sheltered from the sufferings, so Krishnamurti grew up as a distinguished Englishman the day after the new prophecy.

When the great moment arrived and everybody was waiting for his crowning, Krishnamurti subverted all expectations and did the unthinkable. In 1929, with the speech held in Ommen, Holland, he disbanded the so called "Order of the Eastern Star," declared earlier on by Anne Besant herself and exposed that there were neither religions nor gurus that could declare or disclose the only way. If such a thing as the real way exists is a "land without paths." One cannot believe in chiefs, institutions, authorities, spiritual guides and even less in sects.

With such coherence Krishnamurti decided to travel around the world transmitting his discovery. The west—the United States—was his starting point.

Bombay, Madras, Saanen, Oijay and London were very important destinations for Krishnamurti, because it was there that the Indian sage began to ponder the most crucial questions of human existence, issues such as pain, suffering, fear, wisdom, love and compassion.

This last issue, compassion, was his most transparent message; the ways of explorations were different. They mostly aimed at letting loose doubts, unhinging fears and dismantling its complex structure.

Iconoclasm and anti-authorianism became the strong points for Krishnamurti, who more and more rejected the label of guru or prophet, in order to devote himself to his difficult but "free spiritual journey."

Therefore Krishnamurti not only investigated heaven from an airplane while going from one end of the globe to the other, but was also probing the complex structures which are inside the existential dynamics of each individual: fear, uncertainty, the future, pain, death and the unknown.

In Krishnamurti's point of view, fear is the interval which goes between certainty and uncertainty. It defined a psychological interval as transition rather than an existential dimension.

An interval between idea and action, between observer and the thing observed. The vacuity is the interval which cannot be overtaken by means of the thought. The thought can only be misleading. Only close observation may deliver man from every kind of fear, which is not sustained by other fears but it is fear itself. Man, living being, observes that thing which is also alive and is called fear.

Man observes his impersonal shape-shifting process and is no longer scared by it. He is becoming one with it. Man discovers that he is not separated from it, that he actually is the fear.

This is not a sort of reasoned masochism but a yielding to our own evil, to our own fear. To observe it with close attention, taking care of it, then letting it go, like a guest.

The observation is vigilant and therein lies its extraordinary beauty. This field of observation opens up suddenly and the mind does not tend to pile up knowledge anymore, being freed at last from the psychological conditioning of a thousand yesterdays. For Krishnamurti, a thousand yesterdays have made the world what it is, but to really penetrate "what it is" we need to free ourselves of every psychological and social superstructure because society is an authoritarian model that attempts to lead us through the words of priests, philosophers, scientists and gurus—none of which has to do with truth.

Falsifications and utopia are the hypostasis that built society, are the doctored product of our lifestyle. But in order to accept society and therefore not what priests or gurus say, we have to, first of all, accept ourselves as we are. The pure acceptance beyond the veil of Illusion is the objective awareness of the all.

Truth, in Krishnamurti's point of view, is not something static, but is alive and changeable, "it therefore has no ways or stops and can't be encountered in a mosque or a church, being either Muslim or Christian or Hindu." In other words, truth has no directions. It is everywhere. For Krishnamurti, truth, more than an individual value, has a religious value. The human being and not the individual is important because the individual is limited to his own enclosed and subordinated scheme, being a "second hand human being," while man is free because has no centre that would not let him reach his "religious mind." "Secondhand human beings" are conformed to society's models and to conventional schemes. Their scheme is automatic and unvarying. Whichever change they may take up will not be an actual change because will always be conditioned within an old model. Krishnamurti urges to break the classic scheme, break up for good with the ancient. Only in this dimension it will be possible to discover the something new which always goes along with a sense of novelty. The challenge is always fresh but the answer to the action is always conditioned.

With Krishnamurti, the strong point is always to observe and act, but not like two separate centres, but simultaneously like a whole. To see, to take action, to listen, to learn all make one movement. Krishnamurti maintains that concepts are abstract categories and none of them may describe the actual thing. To reach this perception one needs to know how to listen and be one with the real nature of the things. In order to do this, it is important to know yourself without listening or repeating what some spiritual guide or prophet has said, adding it to the background of acquired knowledge. For Krishnamurti, one has to get rid of that background as well. One has to realize an inner revolution, not to change a system or method but to change oneself. As a matter of fact none is able to point to a method which may not soon become a new model of enslavement.

With this foreword Krishnamurti leads the person toward the acceptance of his personal conditioning and urges him come out of the classic scheme of his mind and to make a change, a transformation; a perception no longer ruled by thought. To acknowledge the conditioning is a good sign, is the beginning of the de-conditioning of thought.

Only through the intuitive perception of the conditioning may one start to become aware of which issue actually are fear and pain. Through awareness man is no longer a bundle of unexplored memories, but a dynamic entity that sets out for exploration. For Krishnamurti, a man who does not drag behind all his certainties and the debris of all that has been said and repeated is free to discover, to investigate.

In this case he maintains that a man who is sure of himself is useless to himself because lacks that kind of investigation that is the continuous freedom of observing that lively curiosity, that freshness which dawns in as "religious mind." Mind in such a state is innocent, alive, sensitive, dynamic, aware and vigilant. For Krishnamurti, this is the real spiritual mind, which is far from what he calls the "Religious Circuses." Meditation also, in his opinion, does not have a preferred mode, but is an understanding of every thought and its structure within the continuous observation and a complete awareness. The perception, that is, the emotional content, is able in any given moment to deliver from danger. To see and act are the simultaneous action, the movement that pulls us out of danger.

One of Krishnamurti's recurring examples is the cobra in the room. The mind is the observer, it observes the cobra. The scene resembles being locked in a room alone with a cobra and observing very carefully all its movements. The relationship between mind and the thoughts works in the same way. Is difficult to observe our own cobra-thoughts if each movement of the thoughts is not observed in all its dynamics. The range of awareness offers this kind of possibility. It is an actual possibility where the mode of awareness is passive and receptive and neutral; a choiceless awareness.

Awareness also binds with another point important as far as Krishnamurti is concerned: compassion.

If many of the psychological hindrances may be removed, seen and studied in the light of awareness, conversely compassion may be considered the "intelligence of perception."

Compassion has neither centre nor circumference, and may happen the moment when the censor, the observer, is no longer there. The relationship between observer and the thing observed conditions every man's life and encloses the man in a self-referring circle, because it creates that interval which is the exact same mode of escape. This escape is also the "psychological time" that for Jiddu Krishnamurti is the same structure of the becoming. In order to remove this centre which also is the fulcrum, even the circumference has to be removed. Krishnamurti maintains that: "When there is no centre then there is love." The centre is only the permanence of a division. Only by freeing oneself of this implicit division is it possible to deactivate the centre and open up the channels which lead to compassion and love. Compassion is the hub of Krishnamurti's teachings. Often Krishnamurti referred to an Indian legend: the legend of holy man Maitreya. Maitreya is the emblem of compassion; he is a Buddha, an enlightened being. He has the responsibility of the salvation of all the human beings, and it is the exact same responsibility and coherence that Krishnamurti identifies with the "intelligence of perception." A perception that only extraordinary beings are equipped with. For only these beings who by experimenting with, to the very end, their own suffering, may be able to seize the suffering of the whole human race. This is one of the greater teachings of Jiddu Krishnamurti.

We must reach the clear conclusion that the observer is the thing observed. They are not two separate beings. The one who observes the image is the image itself. "The awareness of all that is real meditation," maintains Krishnamurti, "has disclosed that there is one more image among all the images perceived by the mind and this image is the censor. The one who observes the other images with equality and wants to be rid of them. The censor is the central image which judges, exposes opinions and evaluations, in order to conquer and enslave the other images. The other images are the result of the conclusions and the judgements of the observer, and the observer is the result of all the other images, therefore the observer is the thing observed."

So it is not possible to separate the person who acts and the action itself. They both are the same process. They are a whole. The idea of the One is emphasized by Krishnamurti in the awareness of the unity. All is part of a global process, of a huge movement that ticks the time to the borders of the becoming. The becoming, as psychological time, rules over our living and this is damaging in Krishnamurti's opinion. To put an end to the psychological chase of the "becoming," it is necessary to dwell in "what it is."

"That which should be" is the illusory projection of our desires while "that which it is" is the reality beyond projections and the usual patterns of the thought. The becoming is set in the structure of man, but for Krishnamurti it is possible to end psychological time by removing the convention itself. To deny society with its models, to deny time is not part of an iconoclastic rebellious tendency, but of an actual possibility at least to go out of the conditioning mechanisms promoted by the society.

There is not a more honest feeling than self-denial, it is a feeling that removes the models of all lifestyles. To live is to die to every yesterday; to die each minute psychologically, to every comparison, to every certainty and desire, in order to live each day as if it was a new beauty. The strength when solace comes is the solitude and the emphatic listening of nature. The key to Krishnamurti's mysticism is in the recorded works and his "Secret Diary," in his conversations and his walks in the woods. The contact with nature, but above all, with that which he called "the absolute, impenetrable void, the energy of which the universe is part," seems above all to strengthen itself in the contemplation of the solitude.

Solitude has been a great messenger for Krishnamurti. The arcane key of his existence, and the mysterious energy which pervaded him from the inside and swept him to the outside. In Madras or Oijay or in Paris, he usually woke up in the middle of the night overwhelmed by a devastating, mysterious energy which flamed in him like a mysterious source.

The thing he defined "the process," the "benediction" and the "diversity" were the psychic processes of his level of consciousness. These were the intuitional states which opened up for him"the doors toward the unconditioned."

Even if Krishnamurti's teachings tended toward pragmatism, it has been irresistible inner strength which manifested in him. It was the great artistic sensitivity which made him a mystical and genial poet. His spiritual geniality remains the emblem of a great contemporary wisdom which surpasses East and West and the experience of a man who, with intuitions and awareness, has attained the greatest spiritual aim of no aim, no way as a way: the pathless land.

# ALAN WATTS: THE MAGIC OF THE IMPERCEPTIBLE

There are things beyond life which to us appear inexplicable, almost imperceptible.

There are things which extend in every direction, in a thousand galaxies and solar systems, expand and amplify themselves, endlessly. Suddenly they disappear to manifest themselves again in the superb magic before returning into the void.

There are unperceptible light signals and within each of these rises a consciousness. There is music with his high and low tones, there is the sky and its wonders, there is the shadow of night that carries a veil of loneliness. There is the sea and its waves, the meridians, the nadir and the zenith.

The imperceptible is the mystic sound of a symphony. The universe is a great vibration and man is its model, its archetype. There are men which manifest life in difficulties and in the ordinary, and men who manifest the symphony of the universe as it is, in its transparency.

Alan Watts was the symptom of an imperceptible universe and describable only from the portrait of his pen.

The vivifying light of his works is in the originality of his perception. In the subtleness of his sense of humour. The most diverse of nature and of the events were, in the expression of Alan Watts, the

## MAGIC OF THE IMPERCEPTIBLE

Alan Watts' writings give the impression of picking imperceptible, complex nuances in their structural range, but they are explained with such a straightforwardness. It is almost as if they were fairy tales for the reader. And even if the preferred field for Alan Watts was Buddhism, his philosophical repertory was wide. Alan Watts (born in England in 1915 and died in 1973, in the U.S.) has been a genial figure both in the comparatistic field and the philosophical field of the Eastern religions. His horizon spanned from philosophy to religion, psychology, literature, quantum psychics, chemistry, music and science fiction. A borderless eclecticism accompanied his hara of writer in every topic he took on.

The interest Alan Watts held in science fiction suggested him to send forth his intuition in far off future. This, he explained, was the only was to comprehend what could have happened in the real world and unknot those dilemmas that plagued the question of philosophy and science to the great mystery of life. In the same way as with Taoism and Buddhism, Watts rides the intuition of the great Eastern wisdom, and become its interpreter in every way.

Buddhism for Alan Watts, is more a method or a lifestyle than a religion. Closer to an attitude, rather than to a mystical current, Zen, which is in Eastern countries referred to with the dhyana term of meditation, is meant for Watts as a practice of the constant habit, an exercise of the mind aiming to "Turn upside down the common logic and make fun of metaphysics and theology, making them appear absurd. The Zen technique aims to shake and unsettle the individual, to take him out of the tracks of the intellect and to the highways of spiritual freedom." That is why, underlines Watts: "To Western eyes, Zen methodologies appear characterized by a certain irreverence and are cause of worry".

The common tendency of the individual is in fact to objectify everything and seek shelter in rationality and logic. This is not so for the Zen method. Zen aims to take apart this illusion, to break the moorings of psychological certainty, doing so by the means of its principles and absolutes which are the sunyata, that is: emptiness; the anicca, that is: impermanency; and the rupa, that is: form.

As an attitude, man doesn't observe impermanency and gets tangled in the abstract concept of thought and logic so that fluidity is held back by the nets of the thought itself. The mathematical, technological and philosophical thinking takes to this constant impossibility. In the vain attempt to capture the changeable fluidity of the events in the web of the speculative concept.

Underlining the exhortations of the ancient Taoists, for whom nothing is more elusive than water, Alan Watts associates the corresponding speculative thought to the analogy of the metaphor of water. Thinkers which have dwelt upon such impossibility like Wittgenstein, Hegel and Popper were unable to solve any philosophical or psychological issue, on the contrary they only started hypotheses and side tracking metaphysical postulations very far from reality.

Alan Watts felt the urge to make a wave in the stagnating waters of Western metaphysics and he did it with the weapon of Zen. In his own personal vision, it was a sort of exhortative, intuitive valve aiming to subvert common logic and human tendency, which is inclined to reason in terms of conventions and abstracts.

Watts doesn't hold with rationality and prefers an art of "nonsense." According to Watts, such art is a better remedy to the ills of society and its conventional models. Just as for the child nonsense is prone to fantasy, for the adult nonsense is the drive to freedom.

Such freedom is like a safe space where everything is allowed. An enclosed space far from formalism and the useless adjuncts of the rules of good behaviour. An art form or a poem, a rhyme, draft, an extremely irrational joke may be the weapons of nonsense. Here is Alan Watts' formidable use of paradox.

Nonsense, for Alan Watts, has to counterbalance logic and work as a stronger weapon because it remains intuitive and unobstructed by preconcepts. There is a moral issue which is easily solved, medical issues, technical problems, but regarding the psychological issues it's different. To move away from labels brings a deliverance and a very strong appeciation of life. Convetions are for Alan

Watts that Procustean bed that has caught us since our childhood, excluding us from the game of truth.

Truth, conversely, is drunk in very small sips from a cup. As a "hold of the mind." But the fist hold is only a name object, while the hand opens up suddenly in the impermanent leap of the void. Watts describes two visions which pertain to human nature: "A central vision and a peripherical vision, not unlike a spot light and a spread light." The central vision is to turn the attention in a particular point and in a small area like when reading or studying, in order to be concentrated. "The peripherical vision" as Watts explains," is less conscious, is less bright than the spotlight . We use it to see at night and to acquire a "subconscious" perception of the objects and the movements outside of the direst line of the central vision. Unlike the spotlight, this light may illuminate many things at once." Is like with variables: the action of an organ of the body is itself as well a variable. The variable is a process (a melody, beat, vibration) that may be isolated, identified, measured when consciously observed".

Alan Watts describes conscious perception as a torchlight with a thin ray of light inside a dark room. The state of consciousness familiar to man is a narrow perception. A perception that slowly becomes hindered by society's models and the strict social conventions. Only through an inversion the individual may be delivered by society's ills which hold him captive to conditioning. Aging, in this way he will understand that education to the social adapting and the rules of conventional living to which he was subject since childhood have become his anti-education. The inversion may only happen through a process much the same as the one brought forth by the

Eastern religions which bring a slow but gradual healing. Buddhism, as Taoism, but unlike Confucianism, deliver from moral boundaries and conventional labels which forbid the experimentation of spiritual freedom.

Freedom is outside of the codes of language and its abstract assertions. In Watts' point of view, man is already a Buddha. The Tao for Alan Watts is the personified sphere of the elements of yin and yang, the male and female principle converging in their mutual interdependence. Man is nothing else than a process of the Tao.

In Jung's most famous words: "Life is what is happening." Tao is the universal archetype. As Alan Watts said, the Tao that flows like water, the constant flow of things, is in that moment where all flows that everything may be accomplished. It is in that moment and its endless variables that all happens. To make Zen happen is to make happen that moment which is eternal, like with Buddhism, and is no longer shaded by the waves of the becoming.

It's also true that, as maintained by Alan Watts, to make Zen happen equals to not make it happen and vice versa. To live Zen means to put it into practice with every effort, but without being hesitant in action. It is good to reflect, but one has not to reflect on the reflection itself. According to Alan Watts the madman who persists in his madness to the very end will become a wise man. What is needed is to be always ready to defend ourselves, like a fencer or a martial art fighter quickly, without wandering from one association to the other in a sort of daytime dream. We have to be in a vigilant state, ready to fend of attacks coming from every direction. If this doesn't happen the techniques of the fighter will be without the surprise element. Like the Tao, man finds himself in the shiny nature of a Buddha where all is a flow of processes and he himself is an essential part of this flow.

Being part of this movement man attains the idea of returning to primordial unity, something which he had realized before only in rare sparks. By re-uniting with the Brahman, which is the universal source of the all, we find again the experience of the jivan mukta of the great Vedic scriptures and the Upanishad. The jivan mukta is the one "freed in life," he who moves on the great spiritual highway. To attain freedom in life, according to Watts, it is necessary to experience a frightening loss of the self. The reaction of the self awakening has to go through several psychological processes and the endless regressions, but not before having exanimated the conditioning, to reach self acceptance.

Being a direct approach, the self acceptance is closest to an actual therapy. Dualism is only a false model of society and part of the inner nature of man. To live acceptance I life is the antidote to the fear of living itself. Because, according to Watts, one may be afraid of a million things but not of fear itlsef. "Fear", maintains Watts, "will vanish like a cloud of smoke." When we understand that, our own nature is the unknown and the arcane, this stops being something scary and threatening that hangs over us. They are no longer the abyss where we are falling in, but the base on which we do actions and live, think and feel. "But beyond this is to realize that we do not lean on this unknown, nor we float on it in the fragile boat of our body; is to realize that this unknown is ourselves." The magic is in us. Therefore both in birth as in death, in the creation as in the undoing, in the acceptance and in the escape, life always manifests its magic, either we want it or not.

Alan Watts' life is shrouded in a magical meaning, one that seemed lost but that in the sensitive, artistic shrewdness which is his eclectic genius, finds its multi-faceted, authentic dimension beyond every representation and manifestation.

# THE BIZARRE UNIVERSE OF ALAN WATTS, THE INTUITIVE KNOWLEDGE OF KRISHNAMURTI

An eclectic and world-wide figure in the cultural exchange between East and the West, Alan Watts has revealed as a true interpreter of the authenticity and the human expression as individualty of the man Zen.

Doubtlessly Watts has inspired many Zen followers and artists of the twentieth century.

He, more than any other artist, has sketched the true picture of human existence, perceived with his personal insight.

Alan Watts' talent is unsurpassable. He approaches the most different topics with perspicacity and irony. This eclectic philosopher always finds a way of touching the sensibility of the reader with transparent simplicity.

He finds urgent expression for opinions and ideas in a universe far too bizarre to be taken for granted by common mortals. But Alan Watts' universe of ideas and perceptions is very much extraordinary, encompassing, borderless, imperceptible and mysterious.

Analyzing conventions and freeing them from the structures of the language, Watts takes the liberty to turn over common metaphysical logic, to make fun of science and religion, shaking the reader and taking him out of the tracks of intellect.

Non-sense becomes, for Watts, the weapon unsheathed against the labels of systematic and rational thought.

Non-sense is always his battle cry, the unconventional flag which protects the exceptionality and the simplicity of the individual from the mediocre and conventional tendency. Alan Watts as anti-conventional artist searches for, above all, in the Tao, the unseizable current of the universe. He breaks through the fixed categories of thought which are always coercive, to wave the zen intuition. The free entrance where Watts takes the reader is fluidity. A fluidity which never stops, just like water.

The stillness is made by the metaphysical and philosophical thought. This approach stays conventional, an idealism.

Philosophers such as Hegel, Wittengstein, Popper, and Descartes, have only asserted postulates and absolutes which were misleading, to say the least. Interpretative paradigms and indisputable logics were foremost in the evolution of the philosophical course. Fluidity, as a meaningful, elusive concept, has always escaped these well-known philosophers who attempted to attain the impossible. In Watts' words: "To keep the mountains doing with out the valleys" or trying to catch water itself. Fluidity, like water, may not be grasped by any sort of speculation. These realisations underlined by Watts not only subvert the common, logical tendency of man but even the complex system of generalisations and conventions upon which society is founded. Alan Watts seemingly fights against a sort of regime, one which keeps the individual in check.

Taking up the Chuang Tzu's Taoist metaphor, Watts re-espouses the concept of adaptation. "When we are too short, we are stretched, when we are too long we are shortened. But when this self adapting process has lasted long enough, we need to let it go." Alan Watts seems willing to find a remedy to conformism and the adaptation that has always been working for "the norm."

Adaptation to the norm is, in Watts' opinion, both a hallucination and the worst presumption of our society. A totalitarian regime from which we attempt to escape in spite of all the benefits.

Watts speaks also against the power of automatic control and with cybernetics. It may be attempted to control ourselves but when starts the control on the process of control itself then we are truly trapped.

Watts closely examines such a process and urges the reader to follow another direction, one without aim or destination. The zen direction. The concept of non-action, commonly used by Taoists as a way to accept life, means to overcome all difficulties and therefore reach the doors of Zen, the entrance to liberation.

Watts interprets a kind of liberation which is outside of the institutional models and therefore closest to a spiritual way. His reprimand is to follow this way and make it part of a way of life which adheres to truth. The style that he brought forth and experienced in the fascination of his disquisitions and his surprising intuitions.

Alan Watts and Jiddu Khrishnamurti both have opened a breach in the wall, as Aldous Huxley would say. A border with the infinite in perceptive, sensorial terms— one has found in Eastern mysticism the raison d'etre of existence, the other finds solitude there, opening the way to intuitive awareness. They both have made moves in the still waters of the common philosophical and religious trends through the insight of non-plasmable fluidity.

ALL FLOWS somewhere in a universe which is not ours but a part of us, a place where all flows like water.

Truth has no paths, which means free research in self awareness.

The real reason why men talk on and on, desiring and locking themselves in a endless nationalism, in a self-referential egoism, is because, as Krishnamurti would say, they never explored their own self-awareness.

A choiceless awareness, without judgements or evaluations. In this state only the field of observation counts. An observation that reaches perception instantaneously and frees one from encoded vision of the untruth, frees from fears, distortions and worries; from psychological uncertainties. It frees from the monotony of becoming and the obsession of time and pain. It frees from "what it should be" and allows the pragmatism of "that which it is." Only the perception annihilates the thought that returns in his intrusive and persuasive meaning, and may free from time which controls our lives, hypnotised in the structure of becoming. This becoming, this "psychological time," is an interval; in this interval we suffer because we hang between "what it is" and "what it should be."

The awareness of existence of these two possibilities witnesses, in the urgings of Khrishnamurti, the actual victory of the being against the utopia, deceitful kingdom of the psychological becoming. In this transition, it is like there are two blocks: ordinary consciousness on one side, and unified self-awareness on the other.

When the individual accepts the changing of things he becomes more perceptive; that is, develops inner self-awareness that is the ambivalent. In the state of indifference, there is a cosmic truth that overcomes all other truths and is identified with the radiant face of the Buddha.

The enlightened awareness is the source of the real nature of the human being.

In the state of indifference, all alternates because nothing is static, but moves. A movement, "a tide that comes in and comes out," as Khrishnamurti maintains, "a movement, a unique, vast movement without limits, which flows and reflows."

Water represents the shapeless totality before whose elusive and unknowable mystery, stood both the impartial and vivid Khrishnamurti and the bold and clever Alan Watts, each dealing his genial intuitions and smart interpretations.

# CHUANG TZU:
# AN ANTI-CONVENTIONAL
# GENIUS

The works of Chuang Tzu, the pearl of Ancient Chinese thought, is not only representative on a literary level. Its undeniable fascination lies in the profound contents which go beyond their lexical richness. Chuang Tzu's writing appears as a paradoxically modern work, because of the complexity of the arguments which are debated in anecdotal form.

More than any other Chinese trend, Taoism debated ontological and philosophical problems using a very attractive dialect. In its beginnings in China, religious Taoism (or better Chuang Tzu) anticipated Buddhism and embedded key concepts which would later become points of discussion for Chinese Buddhism. It is a precursor of an ontological and relativist dialect. Although it is a fundamental work of Taoist thought, Chuang Tzu's work is more a book which carries deep philosophical and religious importance. It is particularly representative of Taoist thought because of its key insights.

Chuang Tzu's work, with its great reflective content encompassing the most varied and paradoxical arguments, presents an alternative perspective, one set against a panoramic background where the currents of thought fight amongst themselves.

Chuang Tzu was a firm rival of Confucius, who was influenced by ethical rationalism and determined the course of Chinese thinking for a long time. Chuang Tzu rejected the uses and customs of his time. He warned of the necessity to liberate oneself from Confucian conventions and from situations in the world. By going against Confucius, Chuang Tzu rejected the conventional custom, which was linked to the thought and methodical reasoning of the Master.

In comparison with the thinkers of his time, Chuang Tzu's inspiration was the most irrational. The intelligence of this master was such that Su Ma Chian, the great historian of the Han era, made one of the most beautiful tributes to him in Shi Ji.

Chuang Tzu wanted to illustrate the system of Lao Tzu, and so cried out against advanced Confucian rationalism. Unlike the followers of Confucius, Chuang Tzu uses an elusive and surprising dialectic. Just as a seagull uses both its great wings to fly, Chuang Tzu uses his free genius to fly beyond the subtleties of thought. Chang Tzu's dialectic ridicules that of the Moists and Confucians—his opponents and rivals. For Chuang Tzu, truth acquires more than an anti-conventional value which goes beyond society's present superstructures.

Chuang Tzu's book is to be considered a great modern work, not only because is it linked to the determined socio-cultural context of its era. but also because it is linked to a scenario which brings together all of mankind.

Chuang Tzu's book is a work which was rediscovered and also interpreted in modern terms, because it has reflective and psychological depth. By re-evaluating Chuang Tzu's work, its profound contents and insights into human psychology, one can understand a kind of countermeasure to our way of life. The chapter on appearance and form is a classic example of how the book can be seen in a post-modern terms. Form is seen as something exterior. Aesthetics never interested Master Chuang, who rejected every type of formalism in favour of rational Sophist aesthetics and emptiness.

Emptiness is the key to Chuang Tzu's Taoist thought; it is central to the work and is the recurring dialectics of the thinker. Chuang Tzu disdains exterior form, because it represents the same concept as mundane uncertainty. For him, spirituality is a high form of virtue. Pain is inevitable if you add a shape to another shape.

A fleeting moment cannot be held, because it is ephemeral and belongs to society's illusion; Chuang Tzu separates himself from this vision and puts separation from worldly passions first. He does this with emptiness. If everything which is added to form makes one suffer, then real liberation lies in the absence of form. According to Chuang Tzu's Taoist vision, death is nothing more than a change of form.

In the conversation with the Marquis of Wen, the teacher Tzu-Feng (represented by Chuang Tzu as the wise man of the moment) frees the Duke from his preconceptions and makes him understand his ineptness at governing the state. The last part of the anecdote regards the Marquis Wen's comprehension and liberation. "Having heard Tzu-Feng speak, my form freed itself and no longer wants to move, how far off is the wise man who has perfect virtue!"

Like Confucius, Chuang Tzu has the ability to allude to himself and to make other characters speak in his place. But with the stylistic and humorist talent of Chuang Tzu, Confucius is nothing more than an empty puppet, allowed to speak when Lao Tzu and Chuang Tzu pull his strings.

It is always Confucius who is made fun of in the presence of Lao Tan, one of Lao-Tzu's legendary characters, and the patriarch of Taoism. The ineptness of Confucius lies in his attempt to want to educate men with a rule and common labelling. Confucius' dream is a globally standardised utopia. A standardisation which has now become a reality.

Genius does not play a part in this common standardisation. Genius is not used in a society which is interested in details and immersed in conventions. The "*poefago peng,*" which is mocked by a turtledove, can be seen as the free genius of superstructures ridiculed by the world. The tale of these two characters by Chuang Tzu is incredibly modern. How many geniuses can be seen in different historical eras? And above all, how many geniuses are included in a specific socio-cultural context?

With his interpretative vision Chuang Tzu provides us with the answer: an interpretation far from a worldly society which is always indifferent to saintly sensitivity. The iconoclastic counter-tendency of Chuang Tzu towards his society is expressed in the paradox of the last genius, unknown in a world of complex and banal standardisation. Paradox is a subtle weapon, an emblem of acute simplicity. Paradox is an irrational weapon in opposition to the codes of rational superstructure which tend to obstruct the free flow of genius. It would be like saying that if Tao were not ridiculed, it would not be the real Tao, and if genius were not ridiculed it would not be real genius.

Wu-wei is a Taoist rebellion, the non-conventional answer instantly recognisable as Confucius. A Taoist does not react and so adores wu-wei. Let everything come to its own end. Through a law of non-interference with things, a Taoist dreams of the simplest, most natural and mysterious form there is. The Taoist dreams of Tao. The formless quality emphasised by Chuang-Tzu constitutes an element of Tao. The Tao works in symbiotic synchrony with a Taoist, illuminating him with wisdom in the presence of ten-thousand creatures.

With the insight of emptiness, a Taoist frees himself momentarily or definitively from the concepts of speculative social conventions. Chuang Tzu's anti-intellectualism overcomes erudition by a long stretch – it is more perceptive. If one studies ancient texts one only learns about ancient things. Chuang Tzu's anti-intellectualism was massively provocative in a context where Confucius' followers leant heavily on ancient studies.

But Confucius' work was more than an incitement, it was a sermon which Chuang Tzu warns us is unnatural. Charity, justice and labelling are excessive in Chuang-Tzu's eyes. They are artificial faculties. Confucius was captivated by a sort of self-interest and self-referring thought, whilst Chuang Tzu's work is a text which also offers us psychological elements. It includes not the wu-wei dynamic, which is a strong antidote to social conventions, but also the insight of the absence of form and thus the absence of self-interest. Chinese Buddhism came along later to illustrate these same principles in Seng Chao's key work, which is very similar to Chuang Tzu. Together with his well-known teacher Kummarajiva, Seng Chao spread the texts of Mahayana Buddhism throughout China using the Nagarjuna dialect. He illustrated the problems of the world and non-world – the conventional and the non-conventional world.

The worldly tendency of today's society ignores these principles because they go against society's own sick and distorted nature. The conventional world indicated by Chuang Tzu is the world of vanity, luxury, and the wearing of ceremonial hats; these are all seen as habits and a reflection of social custom.

A Taoist is not interested in the flux of the masses. He prefers to move around peacefully as a rebel, but this is not why he isolates himself from everything; his isolation is spiritual. Rather than reflecting on nature, which is obstructed by a complex rationale, a Taoist prefers to reflect on Tao: the "celestial mind." This brings to mind the *samnyasin* of India, the ascetic gurus who became one with the collective energy – Brahman – by reintegrating themselves with the universe.

Tao alludes to a celestial principle and a universal current, one identical to this Brahman. Stimulated by Tao, every action becomes synonymous with simplicity, fluidity and uninhibited nature. Viewed in this way, religious Taoism has the same value as Buddhism or Hinduism.

In Hindu mythology, cosmic waters and oceans trapped by demons become liberated by the cosmogonic heroes such as Shiva, Indra or Vishnu who breathe life into Brahman, the universal principle underpinning creation. These waters are not dissimilar to water in a sieve, described poetically by Chuang Tzu as a limpid reflection of Heaven.

The Hindu figures represented by devas embark on epic adventures in a primordial era, against the background of Brahman. While in China, in the era of the supreme dominator Shang Di, Taoism had already told of the great principle forebear represented by the celestial order. But the Taoist stories are not as epic as the Hindu ones; instead they are more like vignettes of daily life. This, however, does not mean that they are not full of mysticism or surrounded by the aura of legends. With Chuang Tzu, we hear of legends which also take us back to a fantastical era, in, for example, the meeting between the conductor of clouds and primordial ether. Other legends include the Archer I and the nameless being who flies away in the air, taking a bird out of the emptiness.

The legends which come from primitive Taoism contain other supernatural figures astride dragons which fly over and beyond the four oceans. These figures are the "*bodhisattvas*" of primitive Taoism; they go beyond the four oceans by riding these dragons, another suggestive image indicating fantastic monsters, in other words they go beyond the entire continent known by Taoists. The dragon represents the power of fluidity, and has a positive value in Taoism. Dragons are the only creatures which can cross the great emptiness.

Taoists used ascetic contemplative practices and abstinence, and aimed symbolically to become these dragons. After visiting Lao Tzu, Confucius famously says, "As regards this, I have seen a dragon. A dragon which acquires substance when one gathers and reaches excellence; expanding and rising above the clouds and vapours, feeding off the yin and the yang. How could I have corrected him? I am like a little fly in the vinegar in the presence of Lao tan."

Contrary to what Confucius believes, a dragon has no behaviour. It is a dragon and that is all; it shows its excellence in its simplicity. Confucius, who over the centuries has retained the title of the Master, was amazed by the appearance of these "mysterious guides." The imaginary expression of them implies a psychological observation. Reason and ethics cannot do very much for the substitution of irrationality and intuition — like the supernatural dragons, they surprise logic and human intellect and make them seem banal in the form of stupor and disbelief.

Chuang Tzu had the intuitive fluidity of a dragon – this is very different from Confucius' reductive human logic. Chuang Tzu's work is a hymn to freedom from the social, psychological, moral and ethical superstructure of common living. It is a hymn to the madness of a saint who uses the power of a paradox to disdain human madness.

The supernatural creatures are these saints who we cannot often see because we consider them useless, and because we are prevented from doing so by our own conventions. In this complex, standardised, generalised system which we call life, there is no room for the universe of a genius. The universe of a genius does not align with the universe of the mundane. The only thing a genius can do when confronted with such uneasiness and uselessness is transcend the ephemeral reality of his time.

And if he had not managed to do this, he will have been alienated by his own failure. When, however, a genius sprouts butterfly wings, and awakens from the dream which had made him so drowsy, he finds himself alone, somewhere beyond contradictions and the human lie. As a result, extraordinary beauty occurs. Works like Chuang Tzu's "The Southern Flower" (the posthumous title of one of the most beautiful works of Chinese literature) are hidden upon meeting such beauty.

**References**

Fausto Tomassini, *Chuang Tzu*, Edizioni Tea

# THE TRANSCENDENT TOTAL BEING IN TRANSPERSONAL PSYCHOLOGY

When the deconditioning from the structure of time and space happens, the Being manifests.

This process happens when the Being feels the urge to be free from of the two perceptives, the conditioning envelopes of space (*sat*) and time (Khala).

The psychological becoming (*bhava*) in the norm rules the "non awake" Being.

When, thanks to insight, the person who meditates succeeds in transcending the two space and time cells, awareness commands both binds, khala and sat. Its energy flows in the insight which has as its task the overcoming of the barrier made by the crass perceptive construction of space/time.

This construction most of the time isolates the Being and enslaves him to a dualistic separated vision of the holonomic/all. As soon as the person rebalances the flow of consciousness (*upeksa*), dismantling the elaborations and the crass perceptive information (*krama*), the process of re-elaboration to visual and informations starts. Insight has re-established the harmony with the Total Being. The Being has manifested himself in every model of action. The Being stands in the awareness for the help of the insight, which works as an intuitive vehicle for the Being. Through the process of transcendence, the Being stands once again beside its archetypal awareness (Shiva, HariHara, Vairocana). In such a process the Purusha, the spiritual wanderer, awakens to his transcendent awareness (Buddhi)YS, which permeates the Universe.

The Being is Shiva in the awakening of his Shakti (*kundalini*), or Vairocana the awakening of vacuity and impermanence (*sunyata*).

The Being is the "Presence" who is able to tune into the extra-sensorial reality of the non-manifest perceptive data (*prakriti*).

At this stage of transcendence, the Total Being is master of the form (*rupa*), of the normative categorization (*nama*), and of psychological time (*khala*). The aforementioned process (*bhavanakrama*) has the task of breaking the three envelopes which enclosed the Being in a narrow perception of the Self, isolated from the perceptive external element (*prakriti*).

As soon as the ordinary visual perception is dismantled, the Being reflects his archetype in the substrate of the archetypal eidetic experiences (Realms of Brahma); in the Vedanta this experience is called "Witness."

If the archetype is not consolidated, the Being is re-circumscribed in the form and space/time envelopes which confine him in Himself (*purusha*). This kind of dualistic experience sharply separates the purusha (the spiritual wanderer) from the prakriti (nature-substance), as in the Sankhya dualism. If the deconstruction and the transcendence last for a long time, there comes a closeness with the Ishvara and the following identification of the configurative scheme of the sensorial archetypal image (Shiva, HariHara, Vairocana) and its attributes. If this doesn't happen, the Purusha pulls back because the vision does not follow the conscious realization of the archetype. The contraction works as another envelope for the purusha, who is then confined in the cells of space/time and name/form. The structure *(purusha)* is subject to psychotic borderline syndromes. The border is marked in his own structure. The borderline psychotic did not reach the separation-individuation on a physical-mental level, while the spiritual/borderline failing the separation-individualization process fails to join in with the archetype (Ishwara) on a transpersonal level.

As a matter of fact, in such composite universal structures the archetype is present but their perception of the "Archetypal Presence" is absent or dissociated.[1] If the Being re-establishes the harmony with the archetype, the presence (Shiva, HariHara, Vairocana) awakens to the non-form, the original freedom, of all the observable events.

Wilber K., J. Engler, D. P. Brown. 1986. *Transformation of Consciousness: conventional and contemplative perspectives on development*. Boston and London: Shambhala.

# Toward a Psychology of Being

Bhava "Being," and Bhuta "Becoming," are seemingly opposites. However, even the originators of modern psychologies have used this apparent dichotomy. It was not by chance that Abraham Maslow, who, with a pioneering study adumbrated the great advent of Transpersonal Psychology, and the meta-theoretical methods concerning self-transcendence or self-actualization (Maslow 1962,1968).

To be sure, we may maintain that such studies have begun a real Psychology of Being.

In any case Maslow himself did not dwell on the archetypal dimension of the being, but used it in the pyramidal paradigm of the needs of self-realization and transcendence. Avoiding any speculative theory over the subject of transcendence, Maslow crafted his definition along general lines. He and Sutich, with the founding of Humanistic Psychology (AHP), revealed a new, alternative need which Maslow identified as the Trans-Humanistic movement.

These new currents explored almost unknown paths of the human psyche, from mysticism to trance, from cosmic consciousness to psychedelic experiences.

The movement of the fourth force (this is how it was nicknamed the transpersonal psychology), was evidenced in theories brought forth by Maslow, and aimed at facing spiritual issues which were not restricted in the psycho-social milieu but in the psycho-spiritual one. In 1967 after several meetings in Menlo Park,California, Maslow, Sutich and their colleagues Miles Vich, James Fadiman, Stanislav Grof and Sonya Marguiles were reunited for the launch of the new transpersonal movement in psychology.

Maslow's self-actualization and Peak Experiences (1962,1968) will be readily adopted by Transpersonal Psychology. However, before Maslow, various psychologies had not been developed into a coherent synthesis. Indeed it is by adopting the position of the Humanistics that the Transpersonal movement will go forward. In the psycho-analytical model, the self has only a psycho-pathological connotation, it does not concern itself with a spiritual elevation or an inner growth of the spectrum of consciousness.

Transpersonal Psychology indicates that the experience of the Self cannot be locked in a psychoanalytical analysis such as that championed by Freud, but rather that transcendence itself sits beyond the ordinary state of consciousness.

Studies over nonordinary states of consciousness have been Stanislav Grof's greatest contribution. He placed the so called COEX systems (Condensed Experiences,

Grof 1975,1985,1988,2000) in the new cartography of the psyche, including the four Basic Perinatal Matrices (BPMs four experiential patterns or thematic clusters, Grof, 1988,2000).

The COEX is nothing more than experiences which hinder the realization or the structuralisation of the Self. The formation of the Self may be hindered by the COEX which could block the process of self-actualization (Self Actualization, SA in Maslow 1962,1968).

Actually, situations marked as pathological are nothing more than expressions and manifestations of the dynamicity of the psyche, and according to Grof, the psyche itself could use the COEX systems as means of self-healing (Grof & Grof 1989). Many theoretical and metatheoretical scholars are working to outlay a full spectrum of consciousness and of human development. Ken Wilber, one of those, represents a synthesis of thought within evolutionistic theories, of science, philosophies, metaphysics, developmental psychologies, and dynamic psychology (Wilber 1977,1980,1981,1989,2000).

Wilber's contribution has provided the best holistic approach after those of Gestalt and of the Eastern philosophies. Wilber is the neo-founder of the Integral Psychology, his theory of "holons" defined a "holarchy" in systems or fulcrums of transitions, surpasses Maslow's pyramid of need.

A new psychology of being is taking shape.

The being may place himself in the becoming, and realize a full transcendent integration. Quoting Khrisnamurti: the being may "become" only if he frees himself from the boundary of what he "should be." In that absence of perception where the perceived and the perceptible become moulded in one experience.

The becoming may be like some sheath or like a false chase. The being is spiritual coherence or even a perfected dimension of the divine archetype (see The Total Transcendent Being, see above).

The archetypal being is rather different from the Maslowian being. Entering the transcendental the well being is not of much use because if the being is projected toward the self transcendence any motivational, ethical, moral need would not be needed.

However I disagree with those who maintain that a being who aspires to transcendence has to be of sound mind, for many a spiritual crisis are accompanied with psychotic outbreaks and/or borderline.

In any of these states there may be a tendency to transcend. The dynamicity of the psyche can extend to every level of pathology and still transcend all its borders.

It is Wilber's transational pyramid. The great field of the being. Every fulcrum integrates, consolidates and transcends the one before.

From the physical-emotional-spiritual, or better prepersonal (physical-emotional), personal (rational-of the ego)—transpersonal.

Waves, systems, circles and spheres represent the Great Field of Being, and holonic manifestation. A holon is a whole which is part of a greater whole. As Khrishnamurti maintained, a greater may contain a smaller, but the opposite is impossible.

At the very centre of the principle of realization is the Being. Maslow's Being, Wilber's Integral psychology being,

Grof's Transpersonal holotropic Being, all representing an alternative project to the rational human experience.

The new theories may present interesting paradigms which may converge or move away from other theories. Transpersonal Psychology is rather young, especially if compared to the psychology of the depth. It promises new discoveries in new territories and in new dimensions of consciousness.

# THE SIDDHA OF TIME

PSI comes under the category of "psychic powers," or Siddha as they are called in the esoteric Hindu tradition of the yogis. Experiential data come under the heading "Experiential Logic" (Grof 1976,1980, 1985, 1988, 2000) and have intra-psychic connotations but with such powers they assume a trans-psychic or para-psychic dimension. The Siddha, which are perfect in the Hindu tradition, are the forerunners of modern Psi; they are phenomena of the visible threshold which pour back again into what is invisible.

Clairvoyance, pre-cognition, telepathy, telekinesis, psycho-kinesis, ESP, near death experiences (NDEs), out-of-body experiences (OBEs), astral projections, channelling and kundalini are all categorised as psi. In ancient times, yogis managed to model their own body so that they could make themselves smaller, disappear, or even emit other miniaturised bodies through their own pores. Yogis had trans-psychic faculties of a consciousness which had an ultimate contact with sacredness, the supernatural, the divinity Ishvara Shiva, and the psycho-active reawakening at the divine source.

Apart from reawakening in the god's consciousness, the yogis explored the characteristics, contexts and worlds therein. Worlds which layered themselves in such a way as to constitute parallel dimensions between divine realms and clear objectivity.

In a dimension which we could call intermediate, the yogis acted as doors, like Star Gates and trans-temporal extremities, where they went beyond the dimension of time and space. Using mandala, an ascetic widened the domains of his perception of the physical universe. Thus he could project himself into the great Goddess Mother and dance above the universe in the presence of Kali who, like a *makara* in the time, threw the cosmic dancer back through his temporary opening, and swallowed him up again in the physical universe.

This symbiotic relationship between meditator and the goddess mother of the universe reveals psychological connotations which uncover the universal matrix in which man is rocked by the cosmos, in what Stan Grof calls "oceanic experience." Man's soul is fed by the cosmic breast of the good mother, and in this experience unity is undifferentiated in the great uterus of the meta-cosmic universe. In this phase, Shiva, Kali's spouse, represented by the meditator's consciousness, reawakens to the energy of the universe: *shakti*. In this transition, one can have conscious cosmic experiences or awakening of kundalini. In the mural of the Island of Gems (Rajput), Kali dances on Shiva's doubles (Niskala and Shakala Shiva) in a great mandala which is projected onto the universe.

Shakala represents the parched body formed of sexual energy, whilst Niskala is asexual because of the pervading energy of *shakti*. The two extremes represent (a) the body of the domain of *maya* and illusion and (b) the body of the transcendent domain outside the flattery of maya. Both are represented as inverse extremes in a hexagonal yantra or in a triangular star with six points, the Trikona-Shakti which figures as the wedding symbol of the bride and groom.

This symbol is projected into the universe as a *bindu*, the absolute which watches over triangles, the same consciousness as Shiva. The intersection of two triangles symbolises unity regained: the domains of Shiva and Shakti balance out in a unique point, the *bindu*, the drop which shapes the universe, the great mantra-bija "Sauh" of tradition, just as a seed in a latent state of seminal liquid contains the whole universe. If the universe should disappear, it would return to the nucleus of a seed, ready to recreate itself as in the Hindu tradition, from a Brahman regenerated from Vishnu's belly button to the cosmic apocalypse of the god Shiva. So the cosmos will return to a primordial flux, after the great *mahaprayala*, the dissolution of every form of life. It will then show itself again as a creative and psychic energy.

### References

*Sakala-Nishkala*: in Zimmer, Heinrich, Joseph Campell (ed.).1946. *Myths and Symbols in Indian Art and Civilization*. Princeton, New Jersey: Princeton University Press.

# PSYCHE AND THE ANIMA'S DREAM

The infusion between psyche (from the Greek word *psyche*) and Anima reinforces the Alchemical Weddings – the divine sygypts of the god and goddess Shiva and Shakti. This infusion in the primordial unconscious is the expression of the Anima. In it are lodged myths in the form of archetypes – ancient mythologemes living in this phylogenetic substrata which Jung calls the collective unconscious. "With the soul we fall back into the ancient world." A world which pulses with what is numinous, a world where Jung and analytical psychology find their own primordial effervescence in archetypes, the powerful forces of the Self or the Anima and Animus.

In the energy of the psyche, archetypes are set free. So Anima and Animus represent the dynamic interrelation of the divine sygypts of Shakti and Shiva. As Jung reveals, "Anima is the archetype of the psyche." Anima or "Seele" is synonymous with psyche – according to Jung, the Animus is projected onto the Anima, the collective unconscious.

Where there is an Anima, there can be no Animus, and the meeting of two archetypes seems impossible unless we use a coniunctio.

The alchemical coniunctio is a mystical union between sygypts like the one depicted in the tantric Hindu matrix yantra: the diagram which intersects the male-female polarities appears as two triangles, one on top of the other. The coniunctio can seem thus as much in the domain of Shakti, the bride, as in the domain of Shiva, the groom. So Shiva, the Animus, is reflected in the Anima, the goddess projected by him, and both come together in matrimony. For this to happen, the psyche has to project itself onto the soul, just as man has to project himself onto his psyche. In this game of projection we are experiencing the dream of the soul – in other words, the dream inside the soul which is at the same time the dream of the psyche from which the psyche emerges.

"Soul-Making" as Jung believed, means those in the psyche's dream where the Anima is the archetype of the psyche. The heart of this alchemical infusion is individuation or the Self. Primitive man believed in the dream of Venus or the dream of *maya*. She was green like Tara, one of the goddesses of tantric Buddhism. Vishnu, the Hindu god of life, is absorbed in the *maya* of his sleep (the *indrayala*) somewhere between the suspension of one universe and the birth of another.

The soul is the wood nymph or a sibyl reflected in the waters of a dream, or the waters of the Anima. In Hindu myths, water is the symbol of transformation, it is half of the source, somewhere between reality and the unreal. Water is immersed in the soul and it pours back into the psyche like an image in a mirror. Creatures and archetypes emerge from the water as well as myths and heroes which populate the cosmology of the soul. In the cosmos of its monsters and its fairies, the threads of the soul are woven by the soul. It is bipolar and it is equally good, ferocious and monstrous. "The soul is the archetype of life itself."

The soul is the seat of the Self, the bipolar nature of Shiva, the polyhedrous nature of the unconscious, as multi-coloured as a "peacock's tail"; in Shaivite symbolism they make way for white only. White includes all colours. White is the moon which, like Shakti marrying Shiva, reaches the sun. The XVI *kala* is the coniunctio between the Sun and Moon, between psyche and soul, between the conscious and unconscious, between the god and goddess Shiva and Shakti. The polymorphism of Shiva is the peacock's tail which projects infinite rays. Here, Shiva is also the Soul, he is the "unconscious considered as a multiple consciousness."

If the soul is Shiva, the soul is also a dream of Shiva, his *shakti maya*, the involved dance of illusion from which Shiva has not yet awakened. The *a priori* theoretical element which symbolises Shiva is the tormented, intricate and enveloped Self, not only as part of the illusion but also the victim of it. Also an open game in an energy which breaks into the psyche. It is free to elude itself, to be at the mercy of *maya,* or to emerge from it. Shiva embodies the game of the I-consciousness, where the Soul is its companion and where the sygypts interweave in the marriage of the hermaphrodite, the Ardhanarishvara and *maithuna*, the Indian couples reflected in archetypes and ancient myths. They are the original inhabitants of the collective unconscious.

# References

Gnoli. R. 1972.*Tantraloka di Abhinavagupta*. Luce delle Sacre Scritture. Classici delle Religioni Utet:Torino.

Corbin, H. 2005. *L'imagination creatrice dans le soufisme d'Ibn 'Arabi*. Flammarion.

Hillman, J. 1985. *Anima, an anatomy of personified notion*. Princeton, NJ: Princeton University Press; London: Routledge and Kegan Paul LTD.

Jung. C. J. *Collected Works*. Princeton, NJ: Princeton University Press; London: Routledge and Kegan Paul LTD.

# THE TRANSPERSONAL
# DIMENSION:
# PERCEPTIONS BEYOND THE
# THRESHOLD

Carl Gustav Jung noticed that myths go back to a "pre-history" of the mind when man did not think but "perceived." Beyond the rational threshold is a sensitive veil which is not rational but which has a coherent logic belonging to another order of existence. William James and Jung, as well as Stan Grof, went towards this archetypical threshold which precedes rational consciousness. This threshold is perceptible according to a kind of meta-psychic intuition or numinous transition; an experience which lights up sacred colours, magical pulsations, and hidden, psychedelic sanctuaries.

The imperceptible veil is infused with colours, but these colours are a branch of the centre or centres of unity of consciousness which are unlocked in latency. The field of perception, the bubble of perception in which these units live, is a hologram. We do not perceive the hologram because we navigate in a bubble of perception. This bubble is the world, the origin of the big bang. In the symmetrical chaos of holographic reality, one is everything and everything is one in the holographic extension. This is how primitive man perceived things, with a consciousness capable of perceiving *a priori* models of reality -- in other words: archetypes.

When language had not yet split up into categories, a hidden veil separated the animate from the inanimate. There were no distinctions between sensitive and oversensitive, between symbol and archetype; they were all a unit of extended consciousness in a meta-symbolic universe. Symbol and projection constituted reality, a hidden door behind a symbolic dimension, opening seats of the enclosed sacred, the mandala, in the space of archetypical rooms. Mandalas were the representation of this reality, the seat of a living, symbolically cosmicised archetype. Primitive men were shamans, healers and mystics of the threshold. Doors opened in the Star Gates which are gaps in space.

Archetypes assumed the shape of what today is a hologram, mandala or projected reality. Jung discovered a scheme of individuation in the mandala. The centre is a hub; totality of the Self is individuated from primitive man in a cosmic centre called the Axis Mundi which, in myths and religions, was the sanctuary of the cosmic soul. The myths are multi-coloured, like a peacock's tail, reflecting colours which blend into others, the polymorphic divinity which projects onto one of the screens that it conceals. In Hindu myths, this reflecting reality reflex is Shiva of the thousand faces. The invisible world of Shiva (or Shiva-loka) is a hidden retroflex reality subjected to an explicit reality, the objective world made of models of perception. Primitive man perceived beyond the veil of maya, an object of philosophical speculations but an inter-subjective reality, paradoxically unreal and real at the same time.

Threads of life in the jumpers of the absolute. Prehistoric man believed in gods, venerating them with sacrificial rituals. Sacrifice was a cosmic ritual enacted by mystics, yogis, shamans and rishis - inhabitants of cosmogonic dimensions, inhabitants of a reality that we dare to call primitive but which draw on intimate contact with spirituality.

Mystics, Quaballah, Spheres, Quasar, Mandalas and holograms are the models of the evolution of a trans-psychic, transpersonal consciousness, projected beyond the threshold, populated by gods and governed by an unconscious which is still reflected in the mystic consciousness. There were neither clear boundaries nor oppositions. The unconscious was a place inhabited by men and saints, prophets and shamans. The models of the evolution of trans-psychic consciousness are modelled on the sacredness of hetero-spatial configurations. Mandala and Yantra were the sacred, untouchable enclosures, seats of the archetype one split into more archetypes, sacred guardians or a marriage couple (*maithuna*). Primitive man perceived and explored the Star Gates of the universe. They assumed the shape of the Star Gates' stellar constellations, doors which bridged the threshold from one dimension to another. There is an ancestral, trans-psychic dimension, the door concealed behind the dimensions, the polling station of the real divinity Ishadeva, the real nature of Shiva.

Shiva, the sacred and mystic source, moulds reality and covers it in a veil of dream. We are all sleeping, but only Shiva can set fire to the veil with the fire of his reawakened, mystical consciousness. With yantra, only Shiva can go further, like a projection, where the bride and groom are the first to embrace. The yantra is in the stellar hexagon, one of Shiva's crowns, a cosmic symbol and an archetypical model of reintegration. Archetypes are the portals; Star Gates are their flowing doors which open onto the trans-psychic universe of the rishi. Star Gates recall the myth of antiquity, the hero of the worlds; Star Gates are the sacred portal, the mystic perception which opens onto the trans-psychic corridor where the doors communicate "intercostellate" with archetypical symbols, with a prehistoric and trans-historic history, with an over-rational reality, with one of its spiritual, cosmogonic and perceptually transpersonal claims.

# STAR GATE: THE DOOR OF FEAR

**Cosmic Game**
**Panca-vaktra**

5 faces of Shiva
Mandala geometry

*"A dream is a small door, hidden in the deepest and most intimate sanctuary of the spirit, it opens onto the native cosmic night which was very much the soul before the conscious I existed; it will survive as a soul and it will reach much further than the conscious I will ever reach."*
—*Carl Gustav Jung C.W.* Volume 10 Civilization in Transition

The diagram above lists the panca-vaktra, keeping them outside a purely *noetic* context. Here there are projections, accessible only to the mystic consciousness which is hidden behind a psychic and meta-psychic matrix: this is more than just philosophy. Mystic tantra calls these projections the five faces of the Lord, a hypostasis of Shiva.

Analytical psychology and transpersonal science and psychology can find influxes and geometric configurative dynamics which supervise the directions of space in each of these hypostases. The mandala of this configuration is, in the Hindu Shri-kula Tantric tradition, a Sri Yantra.

In *Myths and Symbols of India*, Heinrich Zimmer describes the yantra as a real and personal sanctuary whose square frame is, in the tantric tradition, called a "Journey through fear"(*sisirita*). Zimmer says there is "a platform in front of each entrance and a short flight of stairs which leads from the ground to the raised floor of the sanctuary." Note well: This sanctuary is the same one that Jung described –the four doors are equivalent to our panca-vaktra. At the Main Door, where Shiva or Ishana is, the axes form geometric lines projected in the four directions of space, as the Linga, the cosmic phallus which represents the axes whose four spatial directions are cosmogenetic reproduction of the universe (see above).

These geometries correspond to the archetypal symbols and they pour out as archetypes. To put it another way, they have repercussions as psychic dynamics on our conscious state and on the experience of wakefulness. They are the cosmic games of the mind. An individual is not allowed to have contact with the reality that lies beneath his/her objective, consensual reality, because this sacred door could lead him/her to the brink of release. However, the double background is the double game of an underlying reality, of which the world is no more than a projection or a hologram.

David Bohm hypothesised an explicate order (revealed), recognising an objective reality in it. He distinguishes this from an implicate order (concealed) at a deeper level of reality, whose dimension is not for us to know with exactitude. But the Indian mystics came very close to discovering Parallel Worlds. Through Veda they revealed the philosophical and gnoseologic matrix – a cosmogonic dimension where, through trans-conscious and meta-psychic states, the point of access was sacred. In these states, yogi pushed themselves through wormholes into domains which were not part of their current world but which were similar to their trans-psychic visions. They unveiled a trans-dual experience through a clairvoyant phase (*pashyanti*). They could enter into the sacred homes of Agni, Shiva, Indra and Vishnu and they could adore ferocious Kali through the practice of vira-sadhana, the untamed ones of the goddess.

Suspended at the midpoint between heaven, earth, fire, air and wind, the rishis of India made themselves out to be bearers of sacred revelations. They crossed over the border into a meta-physical realm of a consciousness which looked at the divine. In the divine these rishis saw flimsy worlds, woven with traces of sacredness, where cosmogonic heroes fought together against terrible demons, sons of the cosmic Night.

The four doors or configurative axes, whose projections influence us like energetic dynamics, act as karmic agents based on an individual's behaviour. Metaphorically, if this door of release is not glimpsed, it acts as a karmic prisoner. The four doors are in ambivalence of the prisons. The panca-vaktra are more than dynamics, they are karmic Star Gates (*kancuka*), or wormholes of a holographic domain.

Star Gates are doors which open onto parallel dimensions which play with the interface between our world and the flimsy world of Shiva (Shiva-loka). If universal reality is Shiva, we can deduce that the Cosmic Game, duality, release, entrapment and the traps of the mind, are no more than Shiva, who jousts with his cosmic projection. The panca-vaktra, invisible configurations, unfortunately underlie the domain of illusion. According to my hypothesis, karmic actions which determine samsara can modify the geometric alignments of the configurations. If these segments, which are projected into space, are modified by an individual's actions according to a karma, there is a reconfiguration. If the configuration is really deconstructed, if the geometric axial lines are taken apart, nothing remains but the central point (*bindu*) and so one manages to release oneself (*moksha*).

*Diego Pignatelli Spinazzola*

The configurations can be square, triangular, rhomboid, quadrilateral, rectangular, hexagonal, pentagonal or circular in shape. Their central axis is Shiva Anashrita, a point without any karmic conditioning. The geometric alchemy of symbols represented in the configuration of a mandala releases its dynamic on the basis of the karmic reserves of the individual, allowing them as much freedom as slavery. Thus samsara and nirvana are geometric configurations of spatial axes. If the configurations change, there is a different karmic matrix and so the individual experiences a different cosmic game.

We can deduce that if there is no configuration whatsoever, the karma is annihilated and in short there will be, as described in Mahayana Buddhism, the prospect of a nirvana without residual. If this does not happen, another reconfiguration will be triggered and a new rebirth with appropriate karmic laws and new modes of life will take place.

# LILA: THE COSMIC HIDE AND SEEK

The being takes the shape of the deity in a joint game of bi-dimensional archetypes that, in continuous cosmic cycles, tend to merge in the polyvalent, interdependent energies of Shiva and Shakti. The ultimate end of the cosmic process and of its evolution is the re-appropriation, or mystical union, where the two forces crash. Shiva, here metaphorically represented as a blazing meteor, collides against the cosmic triangle (*navayoni*) and enters in the temporal flux of the goddess, overtaking it and conquering Kali's fury. The yoni of the goddess opens up to the Groom like a cosmic corner.

Space and time represent the psychological sheaths symbolized by Kali, the Shakti of the divine. This feminine deity is the attractor of time. She keeps the stronghold on the existences in her temporal weaves.

In Tantric texts and in the hymns (*mangalas*), Kali has the form of a salamander (*candimangala*) so that the tentacles of the goddess take hold of time and keep up the illusion of maya.

Shiva is symbolized by the awakening mystic consciousness; by the divine who beholds his own creature, time, as a potter beholds the lathe. If time is immobile, Shiva is ready to set it in motion, with his dynamic activity as emanator, who unfolds the phenomenic existence, and destroyer of the universe.

Time regenerates itself only through Shiva. The Bride awaits the Groom in order to start again the universal creation.

The psychological time will run its course, in this troubled human existence that is unaware of the light of the divine. This will go on until He will not be awakened to the Goddess, until the consciousness will not wake up from the slumber of maya.

Kali's game of waiting is the same as the wait of psychological time (kalakala) which devours everything. In fact, in Hindu iconography, Kali is the devourer of corpses killed on the battlefield (*kshetra*), while here Shiva is Mahapetra, the Great Cadaver. In this tale, Shiva pretends to be a corpse in order to extinguish Kali's fury, who here has the task of reanimating her husband by reactivating his body. The iconographic representation recalls the symbiotic collaboration between Kali and Shiva.

Shiva, divine light, in this form is light (*prakasha*) which animates thought-time (*vimarsha*).

These two elements constitute the play (*lila*), the entire cosmic game of hide and seek. The Yogi sees the deception of maya and contemplates the divine manifestations as lila. He has overcome every dualism (*advaita*), every differentiation (*vikalpa*), and has reached the Great Mantra, the Universal I. This non-conventional reality, the Mantra of Awareness (*Sada-Shiva*) is the first spark of the divine, but it has to assimilate other flames in order to become one whole fire, one energy: this is Shiva.

The degree of Sada Shiva, first stage, wakes up to the whole spectrum of consciousness (*Shakti*). As he visualizes the wheel made of fire of the forces (*Shakti*), the yogi enters the Great Yantra.

The yantra is a bi-dimensional figure, engine of the mandala, and, like the navayonis, represents the cosmic triangle, reflection of the divine.

The transfiguration where the yogi awakens to the luminous consciousness (*Shiva-Tattva*) reaches the remaining degrees of Shiva, and entering above the temporal flux of space and time, has to unmake it in the light of cosmic awareness (*buddhi*).

In this game of yantras, in this reintegration via mandala where the universe extends endlessly in many shapes, the path of human and sub-human existence is accomplished in every stage of creation. To recognize the game play (*lila*) means to reach over the phenomenic, temporal and extra-temporal manifestations.

It is the task of the yogi to get move away from the sheaths of space and time in order to see again the divine flow.

This human epoch, its history, its tragedy comes from a hidden illusion, the world – the mayic reflex (*vimarsha*) of the deity. Shiva also has to reach out to the meditating one, help him out of samsara, the circle of transmigrations. Shiva has to become man in the last desperate cry. This cry has to vibrate within Shiva (*spanda*) so that this early symptom (*sada-shiva*) may explode in the fire of the awakened consciousness of the great Bhairava (a hypostasis of Shiva).

In this cogitation the thought "wants to be thought," so that all comes from the fire of the consciousness of the ultimate reality (*anuttara*). As blazing, Shiva comes out of the primordial waters, from the first darkness, and awakens to his awareness, to his own light.

By activating, the divine re-unites the shaktis who take Shiva toward Kali. Overcoming the Great Time in orgiastic union with the goddess, Shiva finds again his dimension as Great Lord of Time (*Mahakala*).

For it was he (*tat tvat ams*) who was hiding, believing to be all but himself. The games where the I hides form himself to be revealed in his fullness. This may appear as a cosmic tale, but in this is enclosed our whole universe in his last exasperation—human history.

# PANCA-VAKTRA: THE FIVE FACES OF SHIVA

In Sanskrit the Panca-vaktra, the five <u>hypostatized</u> shapes of the god Shiva (Garuda Purana 1.21) are represented by iconographic and gnoseologic names of the tantra school. Here, however, I will represent them as projections of one unique reality: Shiva. This is a reality which conceals the cosmic game of interface between our world and the flimsy world of Shiva (Shiva-loka).

1. Sadyojata = Rebirth
2. Vamadeva = Projection or the Divine vomit "vama," the Universe, also hypostasis of Durga, Kali. In Jyestha, it forms a triangular shape, and like Rudra (Shiva's other name), it devours the Universe. (See "Tantras of Shrikula," p.61 in Hindu Tantrik and Shakta Literature, Goudrian-Gupta, Ed. Wiesbaden.)
3. Aghora = Face of freedom, giver of freedom, transcendence and illumination.

4.  Tatpurusha = Transcendence of the supreme purusha. Double *visarga*, unity between the individual *monad* and Shiva.
5.  Shiva and Isana = Bindu, the point of supreme, non-dual transcendence.

## THE CONFIGURATIONS OF THE PANCA-VAKTRA (*THE FIVE FACES OF SHIVA*)

The five faces dominate the regions of the Universe as spatial axes. They are projections which unite and form geometric mandala. As supporting axes they are the guardians (*Lokapalas-dvarapalas*) of the four doors (wormholes), of which Shiva is the entrance. This is "the sanctuary of the soul" according to Jung, "the door which opens onto the native cosmic night which was very much the soul before the conscious I existed." The door of fear is a mandala or a Sri Yantra, represented as a "sanctuary with four doors, with a platform before each entrance and a short flight of steps which leads to each raised floor of the sanctuary," as Zimmer states. He used Yantra terms to indicate the sanctuary, as did Jung, and these four doors are a representation, qua mandala, of the unfolding configurations.

There have not been any advanced studies about these configurations, only astrological ones, but it is certain that by following spatial and hetero-spatial yantric geometry in correlation with the panca-vaktra, we find the same four doors of the sanctuary. And that is not all: the so-called faces can reconfigure into circlar, triangular, quadrate, rhomboid, pentagonal or "spatial-womb" shapes, according to a specific karma.

Everything which notices spatial influx and the energy dynamics inherent in an individual, in Purusha, the soul which often cannot make out the interspatial passage with the Doors of the Universe, the "Star Gates" and "wormholes" of the holographic domain and parallel universes. Karma serves as an interface between these dimensions which pour out energy loads sufficient to trap or release the individual. This is accomplished through samsaric dynamics, in which the individual is caged and chained in the prisons of cosmic illusion. This is how the Door becomes the Prisoner, the Perceived Cage. The world becomes the objective and conventional bubble which separates the unobvious from what is tangible.

The famous quantum physicist David Bohm deduced the concept of "implicit" order, the universe being "concealed/hidden" from objective, "explicit" reality seen by empirical eyes (see "implicate order" and "explicit order" in *The Holographic Universe* by Michael Talbot. I agree with Bohm's hypothesis that our world is in fact a hologram, a simulated projection hidden from a deeper reality of existence about which we do not have exact data, but which lies beneath the plastic objectivity of our laws. It rules our psychic, meta-psychic and trans-psychic dynamics.

The Hindus had already got there before us, with the experience of mystics and clairvoyants, poets who sang hymns to the sacred Veda. They gave offerings in *stupa*, images and sanctuaries formed by microcosmic projections reflected in the Hindu macrocosm. These mystics of the East were able to open the Ancestral Doors, to enter dimensions which were not theirs but which were parallel and synchronous with their intuitive perceptions. Yogis entered the domain of absolute and trans-dual truth. They entered the sublime house of Shiva, the seat of the cult (*kula*) of the god and consort, Shakti, the revealing mouth of the divine. It is not surprising that Kailasanatha (micro-cosmos *par excellence*, a reproduction of Kailasha, the sacred house of Shiva in the complex of Ellora) is called back to Meru, the Sacred Mountain of the Hindu gods – the cosmic centre where the Axis Mundi supports the entire universe.

If we look closer at what is revealed by Hindu mythology (or better still, the cosmology of cosmogonic matrix), we see that these Vedic revelations, referred to in the hymns of Veda, Mahabharata, Epopea, Samhita, and Tantra, are not of a proto-historic but a trans-historic era. The present epoch, marked by *kali-yuga*, is the age of moral disorder, it shows itself to be nothing more than a faded reflection whose western "false-myth" pales in comparison to the cosmogonic Heroes of Dharma (*rita* = moral laws of the divine.)

The faces of Shiva in the ancient representation of Pashupati, Lord of wild animals, are the same astral influxes which connect the differentiated particles of Maya of the Lord. His archetypal dynamics are held in check by the *panca-vaktra* or Kancuka, which rather than acting as doors for trans-consciousness and meta-consciousness, act as doors of insentience and ignorance. Rather than acting as givers of freedom, they are like squirrel cages for the individual, introductions to samsara, the cycle adjacent to life and rebirth. Their ambivalence is, however, given by karma.

If the configured, karmic axis is moved, another one is reconfigured; if the segments are freed from their geometry they form a new shape. This is freedom while we are alive. If the sides of a cosmic triangle are really taken apart, all that remains is the point (*bindu*) which is invisible and without support – and so we are freed. In short, it is all a question of geometry. Samsara is a geometry, like nirvana, and both are the double cosmic medal that keeps a human being in check. The mental games of illusion are real, but not as real as Shiva, who jousts with them in the "circus of the mind."

The faces of Shiva therefore correspond to the geometric alchemies of eidetic reflections and archetypal constellations. The faces are linked to the psychic dynamic with the traps of the mind which are deceptively real and pour into the state of wakefulness. Shiva transcends the illusions in a revulsion of planes which absorbs all the domains of consciousness and integrates them in absolute non-duality. Shiva has created this circus peopled with monsters and demons, and he can reveal himself in a demonic representation as a destructor in the hypostasis of ghoratara but in short this is Shiva playing with his multiple masks.

Like a necklace of skulls around the god, the masks form the cosmic and mental game of universal multiplicity, and so the games intermingle. It could not be otherwise because the projections (*panca-vaktra*) are the faces that rule the flow of cosmic events in psychic life. These archetypal influxes are similar to the unconscious, which expresses itself in an archaic and primitive language, but they are antithetical to consciousness which is constrained and contracted by them. Only in what Jung calls the "transcendent function" can the dialogue between conscious and unconscious be revealed as a point of access to the sacred. As a way through the door of the great cosmic night.

# STANISLAV GROF: JOURNEY INTO THE HOLODECK OF THE UNCONSCIOUS

When Anthony Sutich and Abraham Maslow began Transpersonal Psychology, it was already becoming clear that in the future, the potential for it would be unlocked. The pioneering discoveries of Stanislav Grof would cause a revolutionary change in the field of consciousness by moving towards a new holographic future even with the discoveries of LSD, optional aids for experimental trips into transpersonal dimensions. This future would be a decisive turning point for the holographic witness, the explorer and the traveller of the unexplored territories of the psyche.

Freud provided the first definition of metapsychology in 1896. This psychology had to go behind the conscious sphere by dealing with states of consciousness. Since then, other connotations of metapsychology have been added, but looking at history from Freud to Jung we can see that Stanislav Grof preserves this technique. He is one of the latest pioneers along the path of this discipline.

*The Journey Towards the Unconscious*

Grof's back door (as defined by Ken Wilber) is a door that opens onto the phyletic corridor of human experience. The collective unconscious is the archetypal substratum that Jung theorised as a door hidden behind the inexpressible. From it, beneath the layers of human experience, this mysterious, magical and in Jung's words "numinous" quality pulsates.

Stanislav Grof, like his predecessors and Jung, heads for this archetypal corridor whose various rooms, to use an image from the TV series *Star Trek: The Next Generation*, are holodecks or three-dimensional holographic fields. They are parallel realities of holograms in the psychic corridor which are evoked as holographic simulations of the exact desired reality. Holodecks are probabilities of the many doors in the corridor; they are no more than "holographic simulations."

Grof's BPM perinatal matrices are very similar to holodecks, because coming from the great cosmic womb of undifferentiated, amniotic, fetal experience, the various matrices become claustrophobic places where the fetus is overlain BPM II and BPM III (Basic Perinatal Matrices). This experience is an infernal dead-end matrix. The matrices as theorised by Stan Grof culminate in transcendence or damnation.

In BPM IV, the final matrix, the afflicted fetus ends where death is reborn, and turns from the hellish experience of a manic, borderline neurotic state to spiritual ecstasies. Here the life-death interface unhooks itself from its infernal BPM state, and moves to the three-dimensional holodeck. By unhooking oneself, through *rebirth* and *reliving,* a patient regresses into anxious one-way states ranging from catastrophic visions and scatological hells with no escape, to hells from which he/she can return.

This journey through the back door of the unconscious is a regression into the conscious sphere. It is a back door to consciousness.

Stanislav Grof called this process *holotropic*: a movement towards a whole. The existential field of one is the universal sphere of Everything. By losing the sense of self, man regresses into cosmic states of being and identifies himself with all things vegetable, mineral and biological. Heavenly paradises and angelic visions are accessible in these dimensions, as well as universal archetypes such as the great goddess mother Kali, the sustainer of life who is also an arachnoid monster with numerous limbs.

Where consciousness meets holodeck, doors to parallel universes (Star Gates) open. For this to happen, consciousness has to project itself onto a super-hologram and identify with the internal field of experience. Holotropic experience is a journey beyond the usual confines, beyond the limits of the mind. Stan Grof is the precursor of a pioneering adventure of transpersonal explorations of man's unconscious from the cosmic holodeck (probability, location) to the whole cosmic experience. Grof has inherited this sum of archetypes, which come back as ghosts in the matrix from the collective unconscious of Jung. Or, like liberating, *a priori* visions of consciousness, he has taken the boundaries of the unconscious threshold into the non-ordinary psycho-active. The door between heaven and hell acts as an interface to the matrices, and its keystone is what Grof describes as "non-ordinary states of consciousness" (NOSC). By using quick breathing, holotropic practices, and evocative music, one breaks away from ordinary experience and travels in a transpersonal experience where waiting for the death-rebirth event is a holistic cosmos; a whole field of all events. The journey towards the unconscious is a conscious morphogenetic map of infinite holographic probabilities. If objective reality is nothing more than a small holographic plate, a fragment of reality, the remains of the hologram will be latent and hidden. That is why it is necessary to bring back the experiences which are concealed behind the objective universe of Everything. This is where they lie dormant and we need to bring them back to the whole. Only through immersion in the state of consciousness can we explore this whole in its parts, and as a result find the whole plate in a holographic process.

The NOSC, journeys into non-ordinary states of consciousness, are prerequisites for a dimension which spans the Alpha and Omega of human experience. Stanislav Grof has reached the transpersonal threshold imagining it as a bridge to the unconscious (as anticipated by Jung), leading to a journey into a cave of monsters and demonic presences, and finally coming out into the corridor of regressive, transpersonal experience — regression being part of what is transpersonal. The condensed COEX experiences (archetypal constellations) and the BPM matrixes are indispensable stages for the great return and for transpersonal individuation. These enable us to access the Sacred and make a journey into the holodeck, a new unconscious.

# KUNDALINI:
# THE REAWAKENING OF THE
# SERPENT

Kundalini fascinates many westerners because of its esoteric side. However, the pseudo-pathological side of the Kundalini Syndrome should not be underestimated. Many scientists and psychologists are carrying out research in order to decipher the great mystery of the "serpentine soul". However, Stanislav Grof's team takes things one step further. Stanislav Grof has identified a personal crisis of reawakening in this "serpentine power" (Avalon). he defines this as Spiritual Emergency (Grof 1989).

Kundalini is a process of reawakening which could take months or years; it is accompanied by symptoms of destabilisation of the subject. Nevertheless, the Kundalini Syndrome includes a real transpersonal crisis, and those who study it admit that the state of kundalini is due to a prolonged, intense spiritual exercise such as yoga, or is a result of past experiences and brushes with death. In each case, kundalini acts as a real and personal pseudo-pathological reawakening which, if wrongly diagnosed or badly interpreted, could be confused with the pathology of depressive or borderline psychoses.

The symptoms of kundalini are of a physiological or psychotic order, and one cannot reject the hypothesis of its strong similarity with schizophrenia. However, trying to suppress the source of this crisis could be risky and could lead the patient straight to death. More research is needed, as supported by C. G. Jung, one of the first pioneers to distinguish a self-healing symptom in kundalini in correlation with the process of what he defines as individuation. Research into *mandala* and their psychological meanings induced Jung to interpret kundalini as a phase or a creative power of reintegration and transfiguration (C. G. Jung 1932).

In Hindu myths, transfiguration is emphasised by the dynamic reawakening of Shiva, the god of the cosmic dance and the groom who, by marrying his bride the goddess Shakti, favours kundalini. The reawakening state happens in phases and by degrees. These are called *chakra*, the points of reawakening situated in the body along the backbone. This is where the power of the serpent lies. This power is latent in each individual but can be reawakened at any time, especially if stimulated by what Jung defines as "figurative, aesthetic images", a drawing of the mandala, for example, where one accesses a superior, transcendent phase.

More than a psychosis, kundalini is a reawakening to the transcendence of the mystic-psycho-spiritual matrix, and transpersonal psychology, contrary to orthodox psychiatry, is not far away. The symptoms of kundalini are of a physiological nature: trembling, tingling sensations, a change in heartbeat, involuntary sudden movements of the body, spasms, cramps, depersonalisation, depression and an altered breathing rate. If someone is affected by kundalini he/she may feel suffocated or can barely manage to breathe. This is the result of "pre-yoga" phases, in other words prolonged breathing exercises (*samadhi*), in which the present karma of the individual has surfaced as psychogenic material and agents. In a clinical framework, kundalini chould be treated with suppressive medicine and anti-depressants. However, as transpersonal researchers have discovered, kundalini is understood as a reawakening phase of spiritual emergency and, if it is not obstructed or blocked in any way, can come speed the process of recovery.

In conclusion, the kundalini syndrome, recently diagnosed by the American Psychiatric Association as a "spiritual and religious problem" (Turner, Lukoff, Barnhouse and Lu), is a real personal pseudo-pathological enigma. Modern psychiatry finds it hard to solve, since psychiatry lacks the basic theoretical support reqired. This support has existed for centuries in an esoteric, thousand-year old science like the vedanta of the Hindu matrix, or vedic science, which integrates itself into a holistic support in the pseudo-pathological framework of kundalini, stabilising the pranic disturbances of breathing and channelling the energy of the chakras to the source of the serpentine reawakening.

## References

Scotton, Bruce, and Battista (eds). 1996. "The phenomenology and treatment of kuṇḍalinī," in Chinen, *Textbook of Transpersonal Psychiatry and Psychology*. New York: Basic Books Inc. PsycInfo Abstract. 261-270.

Lukoff, David, Francis G. Lu, and R. Turner. 1998. From Spiritual Emergency to Spiritual Problem: the Transpersonal roots of the New D-S-M-IV Category, *Journal of Humanistic Psychology*, 38 (2), 21-50.

Sannella, Lee. 1975. *Kundalini, psychosis or transcendence?* San Francisco: Dakin.

Greyson, Bruce. 2000. *Some Neuropsychological correlates of the phisyo-kuṇḍalinī syndrome.* Journal of Transpersonal Psychology, 32,123-34, PsycInfo Abstract.

————. 1993. *The Physio-kuṇḍalinī syndrome and mental illness.* Journal of Transpersonal Psychology, 25,43,58, Psyc Info Abstract, Accession Number.

Grof, S. & Grof. 1989. "Spiritual emergency: when personal transformation becomes a crisis," *New Consciousness Reader.* Los Angeles: J. P. Tarcher.

Grof, & Grof.. 2000. *The Stormy search for the Self.* New York: Perigee Tarcher, Los Angeles: (Putnam Publication).

Hansen, G. 1995. *Schizophrenia or Spiritual Crisis? "On Raising the Kundalini" and its diagnostic classification.* Weekly Journal of Danish Medical Association.

Jung, C. G. 1996. The Psychology of Kundalini Yoga: Notes of the Seminar Given in 1932

Princeton, N.J.: Princeton University Press., Sonu Shamdasani (ed).

Bentov, I. 1990. *Micromotion of the Body as a Factor in Development of the Nervous System*, in White J. edt.

White, J.1990. *Kundalini Evolution and Enlightenment.* New York: Paragon House.

# MANDALA:
# THE HOLOGRAPHIC
# RECEPTACLE

A mandala is a cosmological and cosmogonic receptacle shown as a lotus flower with eight petals, or by a double triangle. In Shaivite images this latter is represented by the god Shiva and his consort Shakti, in classic yantra of the Hindu matrix – a mystic *coniunctio*. So, this receptacle or cosmological centre, wonderfully introduced by Hinduism, Buddhism and also in analytical psychology by Carl Gustav Jung, assumes cosmo-dynamic semblances which are alluded to in Transpersonal Psychology. A hologram is at the origin of a mandala, and a mandala assumes an importance of images projected into the cosmic hologram.

My thesis is immersed in the latest research in the field of quantum physics, and Transpersonal Psychology . The mandala is also a virtual field of a parallel reality. In Hinduism these two realities are the earthly and transcendental worlds, two worlds which unite in a passage which introduces a new trip.

But rather than uniting in a passage, these worlds can also unite in earthly reality. One example is the transcendence reached by a Hindu or Buddhist meditator who enters superior worlds. The cosmo-dynamism of the mandala can explode like a dancing hologram, even in contexts of collective participation such as festivals, dances, ceremonies or rituals like those of the shamans and so on. But a mandala, as a receptacle, is a nucleus of images which are born as cosmogonies and which are recounted like mythologems.

A mandala which is a cosmo-genesis of mythological heroes – the homeland of all divinities – represents the union of symbolic elements taken from various iconographies. It also signifies acts representing three aquatic feminine triangles and three fiery masculine triangles.

"The lotus with eight petals is the main preserver of Vishnu who creates world stability. Around this is a square, earth with its four doors and the double swastika." (A Danielou 1992)

With Yantra, other mandala figures, these elements are superimposed. One example is the tantric shakti-bindu trikona which is a starred hexagon (a decagon) among one of the most used symbolic diagrams. It is formed by a fiery triangle which penetrates a watery triangle. One represents the masculine principle (the Cosmic Person or the flaw) and the other represents the feminine principle (cosmic nature or Yoni). When these two principles are united and balance each other out, they make a six-pointed star thanks to which the universe appears. The circle which sometimes surrounds the star is the field in which the action of becoming, or time, is practised. When these two triangles separate, the world disappears and time ceases to exist. The point at which the world is about to vanish is represented by the hourglass, the appearance of Shiva's drum. (A. Danielou, Mythes et dieux de l'Inde).

A mandala is a magic circle which looks like a *rotondum*, alluded to by Jung as a numinous reality glimpsed, for example, by a devotee in a host at the altar – a symbol of the Self. Jung believes "The archetype of order *par excellence* is, in physical appearance, the Self."

The experience of the *rotondum* is that of a sanctuary with a gold or silver candelabra which can represent a crucifix placed on the front of a host, or a Shaivite starred hexagon, the tantric symbol of Shiva. This representation of a transfigurative palingenesis reminds us of exorcism, the ancient ancestor of modern psychology. His revulsion of plans can cause identification with the symbol itself, like the cross. The Christian interpretation of the cross is very different from the indo-European matrix. The symbol of the cross for Hindus represents the projection of one into many, four cardinal points, and so it is a dispersion into the indefinite and a return to unity. Even the swastika has this representative function: dispersion and projection towards the universal doors of space.

The receptacle has four doors, like "Gates." It is not by chance that Jung had found a parallel with the same representation of the indianist, Zimmer. There are five directions in space associated with Shiva, the central element of the four cardinal points (*lokapalas*), the elements, and everything which compares. There are four doors because, according to Jung, they represent a concept of order, a reconciled duality, a quaternity and therefore a synthesis of opposites. The implied archetype is a "unifying symbol."

A mandala has to tend towards synthesis. This constitutes the experience of an original synthesis of the *Axis Mundi* or the *rotundum*, the essence of divinity. The two- or three-dimensional characteristic of the mandala makes it an instrument of visualisation used by practising initiates. A meditator visualises divinities with Tara or Vairocana at the centre, and identifies himself in one of their planes to mutate into the chosen divinity (Avalokiteshvara, Tara or Vairocana). By identifying himself in the body of the divinity, the meditator assumes the semblance of Idam (Divinity). This state is undifferentiated from beatitude since the meditator, from this moment on, is in the seat (*pitha*) of the real divinity (*Ishtadevata*).

## References

Danielou, A. 1992. Mythes et dieux de l'Inde; Edition du Rocher.

Krippner, S. 1982. "Holonomy and parapsychology," in K. Wilber (ed.) *The holographic paradigm and other paradoxes: Exploring the leading edge of science.* Boulder, CO: Shambhala. 124-25.

Bohm, D.,*The holographic paradigm.* Boulder, CO: Shambhala.

Bohm D. 1987. *Unfolding meaning.* London: Ark.

Bohm, D. 1983. *Wholeness and the implicate order.* London: Ark.

Bohm, D. e Peat F.D. *Science, order and creativity.* New York: Bantam Books.

Jung, C. G. 1942. *Das Wandlungssymbol in der Messe.*

Wilber, K., J. Engler, D. P. Brown. *The Transformation of Consciousness, conventional and contemplative perspective on development.* Boston and London: Shambhala Publications.

# CHAPTER II
# THE HOLOGRAPHIC
# UNIVERSE

## THE COSMIC DANCE

David Bohm's holographic paradigm, which was taken up by Michael Talbot, sees the universe as a gigantic floating hologram. In other words, the universe dances on itself. That sort of dance which the Hindus see in the god Shiva is a game, a tri-dimensional tapestry. The cosmic game. Even if we reached this conclusion we have to admit that the post-modern man doesn't see himself according to the cosmos, within this interacting cosmic tapestry, but, on the contrary, observes the universe as a big machine. The machine of the Cartesian Illusion. A sort of hallucination which dominates even now in our age, and that which bore its fruits as a residue of a general pathology in this society.

The illusion of the cosmic game, of the brain-hologram as wrapped up in the holographic universe, is a kind of perception which fascinates us because it overcomes reality and fills it with metaphysical, if not mystical, terms.

The brain is an hologram wrapped up in the cosmic hologram, that is an illusion within an illusion, or a reflected image projected of a another reality, a deeper one.

Bohm described a superior order as implicit (hidden), and an explicit (unveiled) order. Our epoch belongs to the explicit (unveiled) order, a reflection and projection of the hidden order and of the total scheme of the universe.

"Our brains mathematically build up the objective reality interpreting frequencies which are after all projections of another dimension, of a deeper order of existence which is beyond space and time." (Michel Talbot 1991)

"In Indra's heaven it is said that a net of pearls exists, gathered in a way that if you look at one, all the other reflect in it. In the same way, every object in the world is not only itself but implies every other object and as a matter of fact is every other thing." (Upanishad)

The universe is organized according to holographic principles, but the hologram itself covers the cosmos with its own shape. In the Tantras we read as follows: "The Venerable Shiva as the universe as body." (Ksemaraja)

Shivaism is a doctrine which follows metaphysical laws, and has its own coherence and its own cosmology set in the Tantras of medieval divulgation. Shivaism is not a sect but a system of thought which centres upon Shiva and his feminine counterpart Shakti. The yang and yin of the universe.

The Tantras are the metaphysical essence of the god Shiva and, according to tradition, they unveil the arcane mysteries of the cosmos after a suggestion of the goddess Shakti. Mysteries which dwell in the mantras, whose vibration OM fills the universe itself, in any one of its periodic creation.

Shiva, the creative artist of the cosmic evolution, possesses many functions such as being capable of making the universe disappear, re-absorbing it and re-generating it, according to his will (iccha-shakti). These processes are a svatantra, that is, free manifestations of the god.

"According to his own will he awakens the universe on his screen." "Ksemaraja" (Pratyabhijnahrdaya)

The universe is vibration, projection, illusion. It is a "cosmic holo-movement" constituted by energy — space — time, which are nothing but Shiva's cosmic dance. But in order to be part of the dance, it is necessary to penetrate our own illusion, to dismantle it, realizing that we are not separated by the "holo-movement" but that we are the dance!

We have to penetrate the protective screen of Maya (illusion) seeing that all is energy and vibration (spanda). In other words the cosmic game. The I which dances on itself, passing through mistakes and traps, until it is awoken from the I itself in order to transcend it in the final domain of the awareness.

Then we will realize that we really have been enclosed in a bubble of perception like a mass, which has been completely wrapped in the cosmic hologram.

# TRANSPERSONAL: FICTION OR TRUTH?

Reincarnation, near death experiences (NDEs), the karma of past lives, out of body experiences (OBEs), these are subjects that Transpersonal Psychology aims to clarify. The idea of clarifying is rather difficult because mainstream and academic psychology and psychiatry, with their narrow framework, are awkwardly situated regarding the hypothesis exposed by the domain of the transpersonal.

As Stan Grof exposes, the transpersonal domains belong to the intra-uterine stage, and go beyond that. In the awakening or transpersonal crisis, there may be visions of celestial realms, worlds of parallel realities, or Nazi hells (Grof, 1975,1988,2000).

The transpersonal domains belong to the whole human race, and posses a cartographic map of consciousness seen as a morphogenic field. A series of archetypical constellations surrounds the transpersonal realms. There may be identifications in the animal realms and encounters with ultra terrestrial beings, to visit their realms as paradises (Shiva's, for example).

OBEs are also part of the transpersonal domain. Grof himself reveals an LSD experience that took him to an interplanetary space journey, in the Prague years, and induced him to radically revise his concepts of pathology and psychopathology. This is because they did not fit in the total scheme of the universe, where the transpersonal is an integrative, holistic remedy. Transpersonal Psychology maintains that the perception of past lives takes over a pathology that manifests in several symptoms. These disorders are only a yearning towards self-healing in, as Grof calls them, spiritual emergency crises, awakening of kundalini and so on.

Another field of interest of the psychological transpersonal dimension is the thanatos, the death-life contraction and its damage to life. It is noteworthy to mention that in the shamanic experiences, death is seen as a phase of transition, as in the Egyptian cults of Isis and Osiris.

Death is a passage to life and vice versa. Life which has its own complex, transpersonal, biology with roots in the collective unconscious, where that which Jung called the numinous quality, flows and pulses. The numinous is the magic vibration of mystical events below the terrestrial Gravitas Rex Extensa. Grof's aim is also to argue over the surpassed Newtonian-Cartesian model.

The holograms are journeys in the transpersonal dimension. They are converging parallel universes, scientific supports for the researches in the transpersonal. This is not science-fiction; this is the theory, which becomes experiential requirement. The experiences with

LSD, the Holotropic Breathwork and the spiritual crisis may facilitate the access to the transpersonal domain. Mind is a holographic plaque that observes a configurative hologram, the world, among many other cosmic holograms; it is like saying that our reality is nothing else than a play (lila), among the many other amusements of the gods. But if we are particles of the one and only God, the integral vision of the Great Field of Being may not be too risky. Man gambles with himself, as he does not realize that the fight against time was started by his own space/time perception. In the Transpersonal, time is a small hologram, which participates in the cosmic play of the universe.

As the relationship between the universe and matter is consciousness – a discovery by the modern quantum physics, which is aligned with the Transpersonal current – the universe itself is also consciousness and this consciousness has its own archetypal and symbolical substrata. The Big Bang is a projection of this consciousness, but there will be other Big Bangs, other universes besides the world of the reductive Western framework. The research on the tachyscope is an ultra-rapid process in the dynamic of the space and time journey.

We will need further transpersonal theories to deduce that our own universe is enclosed in a greater, more complete scheme of human destiny and of its role within the cosmos. A transpersonal, holistic and charming cosmos such as the yogi's, who extends his psychic powers to the borders of the universe and visualizes with mandala the reabsorbtion and the destruction of the stage of the universe in the dance of Shiva. A mandala that, when spoken to the sound of a mantra, evokes the primordial sound before the rise of the cosmos. Stan Grof is the herald of a reality that overcomes mainstream psychology and its current scientific paradigm with his sceptical dogmatism. Transpersonal may be a hypotheses or a taboo, but what is certain is that it is founded on indubitable experiential data. Grof is an exemplar, and like him many others will open the doors to new journeys in the unconscious and toward new trans-psychic and transpersonal galaxies.

# THE TRANSPERSONAL
# SPECTRUM IN THE
# HOLOTROPIC THERAPY OF
# STANISLAV GROF

Stan Grof's broad framework forms a detailed category of transpersonal experience. (Grof S., *The Adventure of Self-Discovery*, Albany, N.Y., State University New York Press, 1988.) OBE, clairvoyance, telepathy, channelling, time travelling outside the normal channels, holographic travelling and parallel universes are just some of the arguments that pervade the copious spectrum of transpersonal phenomena. Other universes exist in connection with our universe, outside the conventional channels. Another phenomenon is that of the Near Death Experience (NDE in correlation with the phenomena of Non Ordinary States of Consciousness (NOSC).(Bache C., *Dark Night, Early Dawn*, SUNY, University of New York Press, 2000.) One of Grof's main contributions is his theoretical and eschatological constructions of base perinatal matrices (BPMs), which act as sequential dynamics inside the spectrum of phenomena. It is possible to have embryonic and fetal experiences as a temporal expansion of consciousness, followed by ancestral, phylogenetic and collective experiences, karmic memories and memories of past lives like collective events, archetypal experiences and complex mythological sequences.

Experiences of the consciousness's spatial dilation as a transcendence of the normal confines of the ego and the identification with people in dual unity experiences lead towards a planetary and extra-planetary consciousness until, with the help of imagination and holographs, we reach OBEs and spatial traveling.

Holographic trips are part of a highly transpersonal experience. They are "holotropic" to use one of Stanislav Grof's terms.

If we focus on these experiences then pre-cognitive, telepathic, clairvoyant and astral OBE and time traveling phenomena open up. At the same time, we come across mediumistic experiences and meetings with other beings or superhuman beings. It is possible to meet inhabitants of other universes and encounter various divinities which lead us to an intuitive understanding of the symbols of the universe by activating the cosmic consciousness and kundalini chakras until we reach the meta-cosmic void. Reviewing these categories as transpersonal domains, we open the door to the great holotropic universe introduced by Stanislav Grof. We can observe how these experiences are possible, according to Grof, in a universe where everything is possible within the technology of consciousness.

There are other universes, perhaps other parallel realities, which are the subject of transpersonal studies according to the wide range of Grof's experience. Chris Bache, professor of Religious Studies at Youngstown University, links Grof's terminology to the experiences of mystical types of non ordinary states of consciousness, reviewing the study of BPM matrices and NDEs. Chris has found interesting parallels in the interface between both phenomena. As matter is the interface of anti-matter and the two represent a *unicum* in consciousness, so the two phenomena identified by Bache appear as a superimposed interface (Bache, C.M., A Perinatal Interpretation of Frightening Near-Death Experiences. A Dialogue with Kenneth Ring.)

The figure of Shiva also reoccurs in the mythology often used by Grof, as the interface between consciousness. It is represented by Thanatos, the destructive and mortal force of the god. If we take the metaphor of Thanatos and Eros, we can construct a parallel between NDE and BPM, between the experience of death and rebirth. This life/death interface is recurrent in Stanislav Grof's work because it acts as a "holotropic" and transpersonal vessel. It is a vessel capable of changing death and rebirth experiences.

If we add symbolic images and archetypes from various aborigine and shamanic cultures to this energy transforming vessel, the experience of rebirth passes through a holographic tunnel – a space-time vortex – and encounters other domains.

All of this is activated in non-ordinary states of consciousness, which Grof has studied in detail for 50 years using scientific research with or without the help of LSD. Grof has turned around work on non-ordinary states of consciousness and has explored intra-uterine dimensions and BPMs, experimenting on himself with the use of LSD and psychedelic substances as a powerful means of exploration, thus facilitating access to transpersonal dimensions and non-ordinary states of consciousness.

The spectrum of transpersonal experiences has been widely accepted by the transpersonal current to which Grof refers, but not by mainstream academic science, which puts spirituality on a level with schizophrenia. Grof is fighting to legitimise his theory which has meanwhile gained success amongst physicists like Capra, Fred Alan Wolf, Nick Herbert and Amit Goswami, who are intent on getting rid of the old Cartesian paradigm which still dominates academic science.

Karl Pribram's holographic model of the brain, David Bohm's Holomovement, (more precisely Holoflux), Ervin Laszlo's psi-field, and Rupert Sheldrake's Morphogenetic fields, have notably influenced Grof's ideas. Representing a revision of the Cartesian paradigm, Grof has filled his books with terminology borrowed from Philisophia Perennis (Grof, S., 1998, The Cosmic Game: Exploration of the Frontiers of Human Consciousness).

One of the Grof's latest books, The Ultimate Journey (Grof.,2006), is a shamanic adventure. It is an investigation of relatively modern studies of the mysteries of death and rebirth and NDE. He expands on the new cartography of the psyche immersed in 50 years of research into psychedelic and holotropic therapies and spiritual emergency crises.

## References

Bache, M.C. 2000. "Dark Night,Early Dawn," Albany, N.Y.: State University New York Press

Bache M.C. A Perinatal Interpretation of Frightening Near-Death Experiences.A Dialogue with Kenneth Ring.

Grof, S. 1998. *The Cosmic Game: Exploration of the Frontiers of Human Consciousnes.s* Albany, N.Y.: State University New York Press.

———. 1988. *The Adventure of Self-Discovery.* Albany, N.Y.: State University New York Press..

Grof, S. & C. Grof. 2000. *The Stormy Search for The Self.* New York: Perigee Books.

Grof, S. & C. Grof. 1980. *Beyond Death.* London: Thames and Hudson,.

Grof S. & C. Grof. 1989. "Spiritual Emergency: When Personal Transformation becomes a Crisis," *New Consciousness Reader.* Los Angeles: J. P. Tarcher.

Grof, S. 1975. *Realms of the Human Unconscious: Observations from LSD Research.* New York: Viking Press.

———. 1980. *LSD Psychotherapy.* Pomona, CA: Hunter House.

———. 1985. *Beyond the Brain: Birth, Death, and Transcendence in Psychotherapy.* Albany, N.Y: State University New York Press.

———. 1988. *The Adventure of Self-Discovery.* Albany, N.Y.: State University New York Press.

Grof, S., H. Zina Bennett. 1992. *Holotropic Mind.* San Francisco: Harper Collins MAPS.

Grof S. 1998. *The Cosmic Game: Exploration of the Frontiers of Human Consciousness.* Albany, N.Y.: State University New York Press.

———. 2000. *Psychology of the Future. Lesson from Modern Consciousness Research.* Albany, N.Y.: State University New York Press.

———. 2006. *The Ultimate Journey: Consciousness and the Mystery of Death.* San Francisco: Harper Collins MAPS.

Grof, S. & C. Grof. 2000. *The Stormy Search for the Self.* New York Perigee/Tarcher Los Angeles, Ca, Putnam Publications.

Wilber, K. 1980. *The Atman Project: a transpersonal view to human development.* Wheaton, Ill.: The Theosophical Publishing House, Quest.

# HOLOGRAM:
# THE KALEIDOSCOPE OF THE
# UNIVERSE

What if this world is a kaleidoscopic reality? A T-scope or a projected screen of different reflections? What if it is the reflection of a unique, invisible reality on the evident world? What if the planets which orbit us were connected and superimposed onto other parallel universes? What if this world is the result of a mobile tapestry which we cannot see as an invisible field which the objects of our perception gravitate on? What if the invisible, unique and true objective field, the inherent emptiness that comprehends (from *cum* + *prendere*) each body and makes it dynamic, perpetuates it and produces it, as if we cannot admit that all entities are empty of themselves? In other words, that they have no inherent existence?

The ancient atomistic law of Buddhism, *svabhava/ svadharma*, says that all dharma (things, objects and people) are vacuous objects from the emptiness which permeates the objective field and which serves as a background to our events. Man has penetrated matter and anti-matter, he has penetrated the macro and micro-dimension, the atom and the sub-atom. But man's ordinary perception leaves him outside a uni-dimensionality and outside the "non-locality" of these processes. Perception tends to get flattened in an average person. Sub-reality dodges consensual reality. This is because of a "flat-land" or a "flat-landscape" (a perception which is wrinkled by objective and conventional objectives).

In sub-reality conventions do not exist, they are no more than a holarchy of holons (a whole which is part of another whole.) The holarchic modality of holons gives us a unitary, holistic universe made of correlations, reciprocal interconnections and interdependence as stated in Bohr and Heisenberg's law (*contraria sunt complementia*). The kaleidoscopic universe appears as an immense hologram which wraps itself around holograms in the perceived bubble we call the world. Ken Wilber, founder of Integral Psychology, believes that our universe is an invisible Kosmos.

As a result, the holons pour out into the Cosmos as projections of a larger hologram (see *holons* above.) Ordinary perception could change if we manage to join the two extremes together and find a path between the macro and micro-dimension. Indeed ordinary perception could change if we united the extremes in the dynamic synthesis of the Great Field of Being.

So only the Flat-land (the perception of being in a world separated by things and events, dualism and interferences, observant and observing subjects) can change. The kaleidoscope of life reflects past, present and future and bends the reflections of psychedelic lights that revive perceptions gravitating in the hologram like a colourful mandala. To observe this kaleidoscope is like taking a medicine which can turn man towards the universe's sub-dimension where he is no longer a protagonist but a participant: here he is no longer a controller of the universe wrapped up in his primordial matrix.

Man has felt he is the master of the universe, a beneficiary and a beneficent. In other words, the individual has manipulated the outlines of the Cosmos to his advantage. But he remains alienated from the false perception of the Cosmos. Man wanted a Cosmos in his own image and he has looked for ways of being the protagonist of everything. The Cosmos is fluid and this fluidity escapes human objectification. This amalgamation of currents, this Great River of Being keeps carrying us forward, but we cannot believe to direct it, we cannot navigate it because we keep navigating it! We are one with the Great River of Life.

According to recent holographic studies, man is a hologram; his mind is a holographic plate which reflects a cosmic super-hologram. The hologram is a 3D representation created with the help of a double laser which, through the interface of a screen, forms an image of projections of what is real.

The concentric outline creates another concentric outline like when a pebble is thrown into a pond. Parallel worlds are born from the interfaced outlines. If we can manage to make these signals coincide by superposing them we can visit other dimensions which overlap with ours, like the Star Gates of ancestral consciousness. These are rich in mythological images and <u>mythological</u> archetypes which are seated at the threshold of ancestral unconscious (see studies by C. G. Jung and Stanislav Grof.)

These *kalpas*, defined by Hinduism as intervals of time, are immovable suspended times which in an instant *appear* as objective time. As William James says, "They do not live in a far off imagined place, but are potentially closed off from the state of wakefulness in various forms of consciousness separated by the thinnest of screens. We can go through life without suspecting their existence but they only need a stimulus and with a light touch they reveal themselves in all their glory."

A kalpa is a cosmic age, 331,000 billion human years. It is the cyclic theory of Indian religion where "the universe is subject to an uninterrupted process of emanations and re-absorptions, which regularly unwinds with the breath of Brahma: emanation is the day, re-absorption is the night." (G Tucci, *Hinduism*.) In the words of the Indianite Tucci: "A kalpa is an eon in which the triple process of emanation and re-absorption of the universe unwinds. Each kalpa is subdivided into 1000 Mahayuga which is equal to 12,000 divine years. The Mahayuga is subdivided into four yuga or periods (*krita, tetra, dvapara* and *kali-yuga*.)"

The last period, kali-yuga, is characterised in our epoch by chaos and moral and spiritual disorder. Tucci describes it thus: "the passage from one eon to another is not immediate because according to some sources, each of these is preceded by a dawn and a twilight lasting a number of years. After 1000 mahayuga, which is a kalpa, we reach Mahapralaya, the total destruction of all forms of existence, a flowing back of all forms into an undifferentiated state."

We can add that all forms flow back into the Great River of Being. It is the cosmic metaphor of the god Shiva who dances in the condensed and reabsorbed universe with his five processes of emission, duty, absorption, grace and obscurity. These operating five processes contain the metaphysics of the involutive and evolving universe. Tandava, the dance of Shiva, symbolises exasperation and cosmic dynamism. In a metaphysical framework the universe is self-ruling, following its own directives. In the cosmic suspension, Shiva withdraws the categories of existence, condenses them into a latent state, and sends them out again in the flux of a new kalpa. Shiva is the dynamic and centrifugal energy shown in the universe. The god is the symbol of cosmic creation-destruction. Shiva plays with the universe and this game is represented by the kaleidoscope that wraps the spectator in the illusory and infinitesimal mirage of sub-reality.

David Bohm, one of the fathers of the holographic paradigm, was among the first to talk about hidden sub-realties inherent in our objective reality. He described an explicate order (revealed) in a tangible universe and contrasted it with an implicate order (hidden). According to Bohm, as soon as an object from the explicit order of tangible nature stops existing, it flows back into the implicit/hidden order. There is no need to affirm that this hidden reality belongs to a deeper order of existence which Bohm defines as an implicit outline. This order has its own superior intelligence which it shows even in the smallest sub-atomic particles. Physicists observe this inference in the principle of non-locality (a particle which behaves like a wave and a wave which behaves like a particle). Observable events have different converging points or one unique point converges and interconnects several observable events.

What is extraordinary is the phenomenon of synchronicity which mystics, scientists, mathematicians and psychologists all agree with. This can be explained by the theory of energy fields and dynamic configuration which are both influenced by holograms. In *The Holographic Universe*, Michael Talbot (Talbot 1991) describes the holographic theory and asserts how closely it is related to parapsychological phenomena such as clairvoyance, premonitions, telepathy, lucid dreams, OBEs and psycho-kinesis (in Sanskrit: *vibhuti*) which is being able to move and shape material objects. Some perceptual experiences of this type are already known to yogi and mystics and form the spiritual and esoteric heritage which shamans, witches, sorcerers and spiritual guides have access to.

The hologram is not a phantasmagorical representation, nor is it a configuration of constructs perceived by a reality which is outside it. This 3D representation is more similar to a mandala projected onto the cosmos, whose dynamic configuration releases symbols and archetypes common to human experience. The 3D geometry of the mandala is represented by the Sri Yantra, an instrument which is used to control the psychic forces concentrating them using a geometric pattern. The power of an adept visualisation must follow this double process of creation and dissolution in two ways: on one hand as a partial temporary development and on the other hand as something that transcends the categories of space/time, like a simultaneity of antagonistic aspects in the only unique Essence. (Heinrich Zimmer, *Myths and Symbols in Indian Art and Civilization* 1946.)

Zimmer goes on to say,[2] "The elements of the Sri Yantra are:

1. an external quadrangular perimeter of straight lines interrupted according to a regular outline which contains
2. a pattern of concentric circles and lotus leaves
3. a concentric composition of nine triangles which intersect each other. The square frame is, in the tantric tradition, called "Journey through fear," it represents a square sanctuary with four doors, a platform in front of each entrance and a short flight of steps which leads to the raised floor of the sanctuary. The sanctuary is the seat (*pitha*) of divinity, its particular "Divinity of Election" (*istha-devata*) which, in the final analysis, is intended as a symbol of the nucleus of the most external Self (*tatpurusha*)."

These universes are universal, composite realities which contain outlines of information constellated by archetypes and mythologemes inherent in the human race. Stanislav Grof, the pioneer of Transpersonal Psychology, is the founder of the Spiritual Emergency Network together with his wife Christina Grof. He is the author of *The Holotropic Mind* (Grof , Zina Bennett, 1992) and *The Adventure of Self-Discovery*, (Grof 1988) and is one of the

[2] Zimmer H., edited by J. Campbell. 1946 *Myths and Symbols in Indian Art and Civilization*. Washington D. C.: Bollingen Foundation Washington, published Princeton, N.J., by Princeton University Press.

major researchers of experiences which transcend states of ordinary consciousness (which he calls Non-Ordinary States of Consciousness (NOSCs). Amongst these are condensed experiences (COEX), the bags of experience of under-phased, condensed or condensed charged emotions imprinted by archetypal constellations.

Grof has carried out work on NOSC, exploring the intra-uterus dimensions and the perinatal matrices of BPMs. This he has done not only with his patients but with himself, using LSD and psychedelic substances as a powerful means of exploration. Thus he facilitates access to transpersonal dimensions and NOSCs. Grof is an enthusiastic believer of the holographic paradigm, so much so that he introduces it into his *Psychology of the Future* (Grof 2000).

In effect, Grof has been one of the first westerners to understand that psychedelic, kaleidoscopic vision can be a powerful means of healing. His work, defined as "holotropic breathwork," is accompanied by evocative music and controlled breathing (*pranayama*). Stanislav Grof referred to Jungian psychology in order to decipher archetypal symbols which are, as Jung believed, ciphers of the unconscious. On entering the unconscious realm, Jung and Grof observed direct and immediate representations which crossed the thresholds of the unlikely. All the events are coincidences, and other things like the pearl netting gathered in Indra's sky. By looking into one of these representations, all others are reflected back at you.

This is the metaphor which the ancients used to represent the holographic universe. The awareness of the illusion of being charmed by this cosmic game of holographic representations is the unique real perception which remains to be seen in a continually regressing, plastic world.

# KEN WILBER AND
# STANISLAV GROF
# THE COSMOGENESIS
# OF UNCONSCIOUS:
# MATRICES, SYSTEMS AND
# MORPHOGENETIC FIELDS
# IN THE TRANSPERSONAL
# DOMAIN

The Great Field of Being or the Chain of Being is used like a morphogenetic field extended into the phylogenetic field of archetypes, which C. G. Jung called the collective unconscious. In the unconscious domain we find archetypes or mythical figures which go back to the prehistory of human perception as well as uteruses, perinatal matrices and universal symbols of a cosmogenesis which begins and ends with man.

Eidetic images flow in the amniotic fluid of consciousness. The BPMs (BPM I) and BPM II are tunnels with no way out, they are giant uteruses or arachnophobic places where the fetus is enclosed in the morphogenetic flow. The fetus lives inside intra-psychic dynamics, human evolution and its events. The fetus relives the catastrophes of Nazism, isolation and the persecution by hellish demons. There is no way out. After amniotic indifferentiation, the fetus enters experiential dynamics which Grof calls COEX systems (constellations of condensed experiences, Grof, 1976,1985,1988,2000).

The morphogenetic field is the terrain where events and their consequences are transformed into the "primitive" unconscious of the fetus. The other matrix, BPM III, stiflingly in the uterus, and BPM IV, are the ending—the contractions and the subsequent exit from the infernal uterus. In other words, the transformation of the caterpillar into chrysalis; a spiritual transfiguration into the outer worlds and the psycho-spiritual reawakening of divine transcendence. All of this is one's entrance into life. In the morphogenetic field, the co-existence of multiple events of inter-constellated universes with dimensions dominated by astrological constellations interfere with the life of the fetus. Here, the Archetypal Figures and flimsy bodies take shape in a sensitive universe, and materialise what is spiritual into corporeal and what is corporeal into spiritual. It is in this transformation without the presence of ego, where the small, tightly-wrapped seed of being persists in an incandescent nucleus, that the exit and entrance into heavenly and trans-divine worlds occur.

In the meta-universe shaped like a large breast, the fetus is suspended in its oceanic experience of a symbiosis with the Great Goddess Mother of the Universe. The fetus is suspended between the cosmic breasts of the Goddess Mother. In the subsequent stages and matrix, the good breast of the mother becomes the bad breast full of black milk, and the fetus swallows toxic substances and demons infiltrate the uterus. It is hell. If it is transposed, this matrix is projected onto a superior plane of flimsy bodies, Archetypal Figures and mythological cosmogenesis. The fetus relives karmic experiences of heroic events, such as dragon slaying or the freeing of trapped waters, and experiences a return to the primordial flux. Man's destiny is already traceable in the fetus – in the amniotic liquid of the flow of life. It is like a network of inter-connected, structured interferences in the morphogenetic field of being. The seeds of synchronicities of future events lie in this field, just as the seed of a fig contains the blueprint for the whole fig tree.

In the great tantric mantra "Sauh," the bija mantra contains the seed of the universe in its potential and dormant state. Amniotic fluid is the secret which preserves life –the victory of a warrior over dark forces and the coveted conquest of a trophy. A secret brought back to the surface of the unconsciousness from the rich kingdom of treasures and golden cities: primordial temples, demons, gods, ogres, fairies, guardians, magicians, elves and towers made of emerald, lapis lazuli and pearl. Children of the day fight children of the night, and cosmic cycles of events are repeated in the life of a unique being, projected onto the surface of unconsciousness. Here unconscious is only a projection – an explicate counterpart of a hidden order of existence which underlies life itself.

The attempts at synthesis and the comparisons used by outstanding meta-theorists have opened up great theoretical debates about the transpersonal domain. If Stanislav Grof's model encompasses the perinatal phases extending into the transpersonal dimensions, Ken Wilber's system of arcs introduces an evolution of the involutive cosmogenesis. If the outward-inward arcs represent a evolutionary trait, tending towards the integration of the "centauric," involutive phase, towards the flimsy, transpersonal and causal realms, culminating in the embrace of the Absolute, Grof's transpersonal domains pay even more merit to transpersonal synthesis, hypothesising and considering the advent of the perinatal matrices in the intra-uterus phase. This is a hypothesis which is rejected *a priori* by Wilber in his detailed analysis of the whole spectrum of psychopathology inherent in transpersonal studies which, through Grof's extensive examinations, reveal a dynamic and experiential interface with the same transpersonal domains. Grof does not focus only on the postnatal biography, and therefore on the interventions used in orthodox and mainstream psychology. He pushes beyond the usual limits and extends the personal biography by researching phylogenetic and karmic experiences and regression into the unexplored dimensions of the psyche by activating nonordinary states of consciousness (NOSCs) through homeopathic medicine,body work,evocative music, and faster breathing (Holotropic Breathwork). In the past he used LSD and psychedelic therapies – optical aids for experiential trips into transpersonal dimensions.

Looking for the dynamic interface, one reaches an archetypal dimension or, to use C. G. Jung's terminology, a "numinous" dimension. This dimension reintegrates the great archetype of the Self and consciousness in the mystic wedding with the goddess. Names such as Shiva and Shakti are used to use the mystic-oriental images of the god and goddess. These archetypes are not only models *a priori* of consciousness, they are universal binomial, they are the dynamic interface of the consciousness which looks at Eros and Thanatos.

Research into reawakening crises in the shaman communities led Grof to consider another aspect or sphere of the transpersonal dimension: *thanatology*.

In ancient Sumeric, Egyptian and Indian civilisations, people were already conscious of a thanatological phenomenon. Without dwelling on this argument too much, I strongly believe that the same life/death interface and intermediary realm is hidden behind the archetypal dynamics of the whole spectrum of consciousness.

Grof leans on the experiential theories of the BPM I, BPM II, BPM III and BPM IV matrix models. These sequences shown by Grof and rejected by Wilber are the requisites of dynamics which Grof himself singles out with his holotropic model, distinguishing them from the COEX, which acts as an interface to the BPM in a way similar to real and complex archetypes.

Ken Wilber still seems to reject the existence of these. In one of his theories he debates systems centred on the mature ego (the centauric phase), as the means of transition and progression towards transpersonal stages. Wilber's transpersonal theory implies that Grof's "stages" are a theory of "domains". One is human evolution, which moves towards a "front door" of consciousness, and the other is a transpersonal regression towards the "back door" of the unconscious.

Wilber's theory apparently seems to be a transpersonal victory over regressive forces in the domains of the universe; man projected towards the Cosmos, beyond the limits of pre-personal and personal confines. However, the real domains of the transpersonal universe are more seemingly those of Stanislav Grof. Implicit orders which do not belong explicitly to human (centauric) nature but contain and enclose it. Losing the sense of the Self, man regresses to cosmic states of being, identifying himself with animal, vegetable, biological and mineral realms. In these dimensions, heavenly paradises, mystic visions, universal archetypes like the Great Goddess Mother Kali and her spouse Shiva, the interface of cosmic consciousness, can be accessed.

In the wedding union, represented by perfect tantric yantra geometry, Shiva is at the highest point and Shakti at the bottom. Both are names for universal reintegration, archetypal prototypes of consciousness which has very precise dynamics and archetypal constellations (COEX systems). By a brusque interruption of the re-integrative element (separation-individuation) innoculate theirselves from psychopathological disturbances represented in the same COEX. Grof seems to be more coherent, despite Ken Wilber's model of systems and arcs (Wilber 1980). A holon is a hole that is part of a whole, according to Wilber. This whole, according to Grof must go back to a regressive state; it has to "relive" (on a karmic level) its experiences which were hidden behind the objective and rational universe of everything. This is where transpersonal theories find their completeness, re-entering a more extended scheme of the universe and its archetypal domain.

# References

*Ken Wilber's Spectrum Psychology: Observations from Clinical Consciousness Research,* by Stanislav Grof M.D..

# HOLOGRAPHIC VORTEX: STANISLAV GROF'S MODEL THEORY AND SPACE TRAVELS

Drawing a parallel from the phenomenological framework of Stanislav Grof, I will draw a comparison between basic perinatal matrices and space-holographic vortexes.

Holotropic and non-ordinary states of consciousness are central to the understanding of a comprehensive model of the psyche as outlined by Grof. Exploring holotropic mind and holographic universes, I will introduce Grof's framework as an important gateway to understanding the processes of death and rebirth, along with the ancient and deeper mysteries of the dead.

We will look more deeply into Grof's work, but beforehand, I will offer an outlook of the holotropic processes necessary to understand transpersonal and collective unconscious and its multidimensional meaning. This is due to archetypes.

*A priori*, these visions look like patterns of vision and behaviour—archetypes that Grof describes as condensed experiences (COEX) and basic perinatal matrices (BPMs).

1. The BPMs (basic perinatal matrices) and
2. COEX (systems of condensed experiences)

## Basic Perinatal Matrices

(BPM): These are general experiential patterns related to the stages of biological birth. These BPM are used here as a theoretical model, and do not necessarily imply causal nexus.

COEX: Systems of Condensed Experience.

A COEX system is a specific memory constellation comprised of a condensed form of experiences (and/or fantasies) from different life periods of the individual. Memories belonging to a particular COEX system have a similar basic theme or contain similar elements and are accompanied by a strong emotional charge of the same quality.It should be understood that the COEX systems are generally sub-ordinate to the BPMs, but they show a great degree of relative functional independence.

The BPM (basic perinatal matrices) BPM II are tunnels with no way out, they are giant uteruses or arachnophobic places where the fetus is enclosed in the morphogenetic flow. The fetus lives inside intra-psychic dynamics, human evolution and its events. The fetus relives the catastrophes of Nazism, isolation and the persecution by hellish demons. There is no way out. After amniotic indifferentiation the fetus enters experiential dynamics which Stanislav Grof calls constellations of condensed experiences.

The morphogenetic field is the terrain where events and their consequences are transformed into the "primitive" unconscious of the fetus. The other matrix, BPM III, stifling in the uterus, and BPM IV, are the ending: the contractions and the subsequent exit from the infernal uterus.

This theoretical framework therefore links to the experiential therapy which Grof calls Holotropic Breath work. Understanding the importance of psychedelics, Stan Grof focuses on experiential traveling and shamanic journeying with the aid of holographic tools (LSD) such as experiential trips. Karl Pribram's holographic model of the brain plays an important role as well, providing a cornerstone which Grof draws on in his own holonomic therapy and discoveries. Grof's concept of the holotropic model comes close to the ancient Hindu insight *Tat Tvam Asi* an epitome of everything. Grof's epitome lies in his extended theory of the holotropic mind—so below so above—a macrocosmic world into a microcosmic universe and vice versa.

Deepening his insight of the Everything, Grof discovered holography as a counterpart of the same holotropic process. His own exploration of the holographic looks like an extension of the holonomic model of the psyche. Pribram's conceptual framework has been explored by Grof, and delves into the deeper whole extension of everything. (Holotropic means "toward a wholeness," from the Greek *holos* = whole, and *trepein* = moving in the direction of something).

Holotropic content concerns mythology and philosophical aspects of life and death. Traces of such mythologies can be found in the ancient Egyptian book of the Dead—in the Mayan mythology that concerns Codex Borgia and Codex Maya Aztec as well. Drawing upon this mythology, Grof has found a coherent and comprehensive model of understanding the archetypes of the human unconscious.

Holotropic models contain mythological motifs and mythological sequences of life and rebirth and NDEs (Near Death Experiences) as well as life after death. Drawing a parallel with the holographic, we will find an unknown source of existence which attracts the human psyche into and within the cosmos. The psyche is a holographic plate that explores waves and astral dimensions. "Characteristic of this situation is the experience of a three-dimensional spiral, funnel or vortex sucking the subject relentlessy toward its centre" (Stanislav Grof's *The Adventure of Self-Discovery*, SUNY Press, 1988). The Holographic plate explores time and space as well as energy and the holoflux/holomovement outlined by physicist scientist David Bohm.

The famous quantum physicist David Bohm deduced the concept of "implicate" order, the universe being "concealed/hidden" from objective, "explicate" reality seen by empirical eyes (see "implicate order" and "explicate order" in *The Holographic Universe* by Michael Talbot, 1991.) I agree with Bohm's hypothesis that our world is in fact a hologram, a simulated projection hidden from a deeper reality of existence about which we do not have exact data but which lies beneath the plastic objectivity of our laws. It rules our psychic, meta-psychic and trans-psychic dynamics.

A Human being is encapsulated in a vessel that will journey into a space vortex—a non-ordinary channel outside conventional ordinary dimensions. Travelling into 3D dimensions, the capsule explores hidden as well as invisible realms, like Hindu heavens and palaces of the gods, the great mother goddess Kali and the goddess Isis from ancient Egypt. These sequences are very fast and linear time disappears, while images are imprinted into the holographic screen of the brain as karmic experiences. The holographic vortex has been activated and the encapsulated psyche travels the landscape of the soul. The posthumous journey. The Atman Journey that projects life-death and rebirth sequences onto the screen of the mind and spectrum of consciousness.

We access the experiential gateway to the holographic vortex and go beyond the liminal phenomena better known as holographic and parallel realities. Coming from the great cosmic womb of undifferentiated, amniotic, fetal experience, the various matrices become claustrophobic places where the fetus is overlain BPM II and BPM III (Basic Perinatal Matrices BPM II and BPM III). This experience is an infernal dead-end matrix. The matrices as theorised by Stanislav Grof culminate in eschatological hells or liberation. In the last matrix, BPM IV, the afflicted fetus ends where death is reborn and turns from the hellish experience of a manic, borderline neurotic state into spiritual ecstasies where the life-death interface unhooks itself from its infernal BPM state and moves to the three-dimensional holographic space.

By unhooking oneself, through *rebirth* and *reliving,* a patient regresses into anxious one-way states ranging from catastrophic visions and scatological hells with no escape, to hells from which he/she can return. Drawing a parallel with the holographic model, we will discover a message from an unknown source that attracted the psyche inside and outside the cosmos. The archetypes act as attractor of the psyche. The psyche is a holographic plate that explores the waves and astral dimensions—the OBEs, travelling into time-space-energy with the holomovement (holoflux) identified by American physicist David Bohm. The human being is encapsulated in a time-capsule that will travel into a space-time-vortex, a channel outside the ordinary states of consciousness (NOSCs) and their dimensions. Navigating the 3D dimensions, the capsule explores the invisible paradises like Hindu paradises and the Great Mother Kali, the goddess Isis with Osiris and the ancient mysteries of pre-Columbian Mayan civilization, the reality of time as holographic simulations (holodecks), the cosmic dance of Shiva and the underworld of Neptune and Osiris.

These sequences are faster and linear time disappears while images are imprinted into the holographic screen of the brain, as karmic experiences. The holographic vortex has been activated and the psyche crosses the landscapes of the collective unconscious, in rapid succession. Atman is travelling. The projection of life, death and rebirth follow in sequence on the screen of the mind. We have access to the main holographic vortex, and to liminal phenomena better known as Holographic vortices and parallel universes. The posthumous journey of the soul has happened. Nazi camps, eschatological sequences of martyrs and torture occur as in the third matrix of Grof (BPM III) and come out in the identification of symbolic rituals and messianic historic messiahs like Christ, Buddha and Mohammed in the third matrix (BPM III).

The desert lands surround the mystical Kabah, with dancing Sufi who dance in front of Kaba and Shaivite celestial visions of the realm of the god Shiva. From the vortex appear geometric symbols such as the mandalas and yantras. The geometric triangle (yantra) appears as the sacred marriage of the gods Shiva and Shakti. The mandala takes holographic vortex and frequencies symbols and custodians of all humanity appear as primitive representation of ancient mother myths. The Great Mother is represented by rites and mythological representations of all times, a container and circle, mandala, uterus and vase.

The unconscious, the dragon and snake, are uroboric in the mythological and numinous manifestation and perception. The Great Mother appears as Kali, Isis, Tiamat, Nut or Nechbet—and is the key to life, it is the energy that permeates the universe and it contains one of the synonyms of Ishtar and Nut in its cosmic womb, feeding humankind like a Egyptian celestial cow. The entry into life is a heavenly door. As in the ancient cults of Mesopotamia, it is the adoration of the winged door in connection with the Goddess, the vessel and the moon. The meaning of this symbol is still unknown (Erich Neumann, *The Great Mother*,Verlag 1956). It is probably the *dolmen*, the sacred enclosure marking the sacred domain of the Great Mother-cow. The Door or access to the Goddess, is her uterus (see BPM basic perinatal matrices). In rites, it is the gateway to the threshold, as a numinous and symbolic place, a symbol of the Great Mother. Dolmen is the door that connects the channel with rebirth. Dolmen is the sacred abode, the entry into the holographic tunnel and the journey into the underground world of the seven doorways of the god Osiris. The seven doors are the doors of the underworld dwellings, connected to the seven "homes" in the esoteric language of the Book of the Dead. In every house of Osiris, there is a divinity. We find a similar description in the Maithuna in India, the sacred couples who stand before the portals of Shaivite temples, and the Dvrapalas, frightening custodians located at the entrance of every Hindu temple.

The reason for rebirth is linked to other domains and parallel universes between one space-time region and another, through wormholes and white holes which connect black holes through a holographic tunnel in another part of the universe; in this case a secondary universe. The vortex is connected with the universe and space-travels within the white-hole and the dynamics of the wormholes.

Stanley Krippner is a renowned researcher and investigator of parapsychology. As an exponent of Transpersonal Psychology and shamanic fields, Krippner explores altered states of consciousness and rites of passage in liminal contexts, besides those phenomena which he identifies as "trickster". For many decades Krippner's studies have concentrated on several frontiers: shamanic rituals, anomalous phenomena, parapsychology, philosophy, religion, science and mythology. Opening up new frontiers in human consciousness and its investigation, as well as non-ordinary exploration of mystic states, dreams, myth and psychotherapy, Krippner opened a gateway to the unknown as well as new methods which experiment with lucid dreams and shamanic rites of passage in aborigine peoples of South American and Native American peoples. The liminal threshold is a journey into the intermediary realm of ancestors.

Post-mortem studies, the rites of initiation, and afterlife as well as the proximity of the god Osiris, and the goddess Isis in the Egyptian book of the dead, have spurred the work of Grof, who has been involved with an in-depth research in crises of initiation and Shamanic crises, Aboriginal rites of passage, ancient mysteries of death and rebirth, Pert em Hru Egyptian, Bardo Thodol, the ceramix codex Maya and near death experiences over the eschatological myths that are also complex and mythological sequences within the perinatal level of unconscious.

## References

Bache, C. 2000. *Dark Night, Early Dawn*. Albany, N.Y.: State University New York Press.

Bohm, D. *The holographic paradigm*. Boulder, CO: Shambhala.

Bohm, D. 1987. *Unfolding meaning*. London: Ark..

Bohm, D. 1983. *Wholeness and the implicate order*. London: Ark.

Bohm, D. e Peat F.D. 1987. *Science, order and creativity*. New York: Bantam .

Chamberlain, D. B. 1981. Birth recall in hypnosis. *Birth Psychology Bulletin, 2*(2), 14-18.

————. 1987. "Consciousness at birth: The range of empirical evidence." In T. R. Verny (ed.), *Pre- and perinatal psychology: An introduction*. New York: Human Sciences. 69-90.

Greyson, B. 1985. A typology of near-death experiences. American Journal of Psychiatry, 142, 967-69.

————. 1990. Near-death encounters with and without near-death experiences: Comparative NDE scale profiles. *Journal of Near-Death Studies*, 8(3), 151-61.

Grof, S. 1976. *Realms of Human Unconscious*. New York: Viking.

Grof, S. & C. Grof. 1980. *Beyond Death*. London: Thames and Hudson.

Grof, S. 1987. *The Adventure of Self Discovery*. Albany, N.Y.: State University of New York Press.

Grof, S. & C. Grof. 1989. "Spiritual Emergency: When Personal Transformation becomes a Crisis," *New Consciousness Reader*, Los Angeles: J. P. Tarcher.

Grof, S. 1975. *Realms of the Human Unconscious: Observations from LSD Research*. New York: Viking Press.

————. 1980. *LSD Psychotherapy*. Pomona, CA: Hunter House.

————. 1985. *Beyond the Brain: Birth, Death, and Transcendence in Psychotherapy*. Albany, N.Y: State University New York Press.

———— 1988. *The Adventure of Self-Discovery*. Albany, N.Y.: State University New York Press.

Grof S., H. Zina Bennett.1992. *The Holotropic Mind*. San Francisco: Harper Collins MAPS.

Grof, S. 1998. *The Cosmic Game: Exploration of the Frontiers of Human Consciousness*. Albany, N.Y.: State University New York Press.

———. 2000. *Psychology of the Future. Lesson from Modern Consciousness Research*. Albany, N.Y.: State University New York Press.

Grof, S. & C. Grof. 2000. *The Stormy Search for the Self*. New York: Perigee/Tarcher Los Angeles, Ca Putnam.

Grof, S. 2001. *LSD Psychotherapy*. Florida: MAPS.

———.1975. *Realms of the Human Unconscious: Observations from LSD Research*. New York: Viking Press. Paperback: E. P. Dutton, 1976.

———.1977. *The Human Encounter with Death*. New York: E. P. Dutton (with Joan Halifax).

———.1980. *LSD Psychotherapy*. Pomona, CA: Hunter House.

———.1980. *Beyond Death: Gates of Consciousnes*s. London: Thames and Hudson (with Christina Grof).

———.1984. *Ancient Wisdom and Modern Science*. ed. Albany, N.Y.: State University New York Press.

———.1985. *Beyond the Brain: Birth, Death, and Transcendence in Psychotherapy*. Albany, N.Y.: State University New York Press.

———.1987. *The Adventure of Self-Discovery*. Albany, N.Y.: State University New York Press.

———.1988. *Human Survival and Consciousness Evolution*. ed. Albany, N.Y.: State University New York Press.

———.1989. *Spiritual Emergency: When Personal Transformation Becomes a Crisis*. Los Angeles: J. P. Tarcher (ed. with Chrstina Grof).

———.1991. *The Stormy Search for the Self: A Guide to Personal Growth Through Transformational Crises*. Los Angeles: J. P. (with Christina Grof).

———.1994. *The Holotropic Mind: The Three Levels of Conscious-ness and How They Shape Our Lives*. San Francisco: Harper Collins (with Hal Zina Bennett).

———.1994. *Books of the Dead: Manuals for Living and Dying*. London: Thames and Hudson.

———.1998. *The Cosmic Game: Exploration of the Frontiers of Human Consciousness*. Albany, N.Y.: State University New York Press.

———. 1956. "Symbols of Transformation." *Collected Works*, vol. 5, Bollingen Series XX, Princeton, N.J.: Princeton University Press.

———. 1959. "The Archetypes and the Collective Unconscious." *Collected Works*, vol. 9,1. Bollingen Series XX, Princeton, N. J.: Princeton University Press.

———. 1960. "A Review of the Complex Theory." *Collected Works*, vol. 8, Bollingen Series XX. Princeton, N.J.: Princeton University Press.

———. 1989. Some touchstones for parapsychological research. In G.K. Zollschan, J.F. Schumaker, & G.F. Walsh (eds.), *Exploring the paranormal: Perspectives on belief and experience* (167-183). Lindfield, New South Wales, Australia: Unity Press.

————. 1990. Frontiers in dreamwork. In S. Krippner (ed.), *Dreamtime and dreamwork: Decoding the language of the night* (207-13). Los Angeles: Tarcher.

————. 1993. Telepathy and dreaming. In M.A. Carskadon (ed.), *Encyclopedia of sleep and dreaming* (612-13). New York: Macmillan.

————. 1994. Waking life, dream life, and the construction of reality. *Anthropology of Consciousness*, 5(3), 17-24.

Krippner, S., & Welch, P. 1992. *Spiritual dimensions of healing: From native shamanism to contemporary health care.* New York: Irvington.

Krippner, S., & J. Dillard,. 1988. *Dreamworking.* Buffalo, NY: Bearly.

Krippner, S., M. Ullman & M. Honorton. 1971. A precognitive dream study with a single subject. *Journal of the American Society for Psychical Research*, 65, 192-203.

Krippner, S., & A. Vitoldo. 1986. *The realms of healing* (3rd ed.). Berkeley, CA: Celestial Arts.

Krippner, S. 1989. Mythological aspects of death and dying. In A. Berger et al. (eds.), *Perspectives on death and dying* (3-13). Philadelphia: Charles Press.

————. 1990. Tribal shamans and their travels into dreamtime. In S. Krippner (ed.), *Dreamtime and dreamwork: Decoding the language of the night* (pp. 185-93). Los Angeles: J. P. Tarcher/Perigee.

Krippner, S., & L. Faith. 2001. Exotic dreams: A cross-cultural study. *Dreaming, 11*, 73-82.

Laszlo, E. 1987. The psi-field hypothesis. *IS Journal, 4*, 13-28.

―――. 1993. *The creative cosmos: A unified science of matter, life, and mind*. Edinburgh: Floris.

―――. 1997. *The whispering pond*. New York: Harper Collins.

―――. 2001, Sept. 1. Human evolution in the third millennium. *Futures*, 1-11.

――― 2004. *Science and the Akashic field: An integral theory of everything*. Rochester, N.Y.: Inner Traditions.

Moody, R. A. & P. Perry. 1988. *The light beyond*. New York: Bantam.

Moody, R. A. 1975. *Life after life*. Covington, GA: Mockingbird.

―――1977. *Reflections on life after life*. San Francisco: Cameron.

Neumann, Erich.1972. *The Great Mother*. Princeton, N.J.:Princeton University Press.

Pribram, K. H. 1971. *Languages of the brain: Experimental paradoxes and principles in neuropsychology*. Englewood Cliffs, NJ: Prentice-Hall.

―――1991. *Brain and perception: Holonomy and structure in figural processing*. Hillsdale, N.J.: Lawrence Erlbaum Associates.

Ring, K. 1980. *Life at death: Scientific investigation of the near-death experience.* New York: Coward, McCann & Geoghegan.

———1984. *Heading toward Omega: Insearch of the meaning of the near-death experience.* New York: William Morrow.

Ring, K. & M. Lawrence. 1993. Further evidence for veridical perception during near-death experiences. *Journal of Near-Death Studies, 11*, 223-230.

Talbot M. 1991. *The Holographic Universe.*

———. 1988. *Beyond the quantum.* New York: Bantam Books.

———. 1997. Milan: Tutto è uno, Urra.

Wade, J. 1996. *Changes of mind: A holonomic theory of the evolution of consciousness.* Albany, N.Y.: State University of New York Press

Wolf, F. Alan. 1993. *The Dreaming Universe: Investigations of the Middle Realm of Consciousness and Matter.* New York: Summit Books.

———. 1985. The Quantum Pshysics of Consciousness: Towards a New Psychology, "Integrative Psychology", vol. 3, 236-47; 1989. On the Quantum Physical Theory of Subjective Antedating, "Journal of Theoretical Biology", vol. 136, 13-19.

———. 1981. *Taking the Quantum Leap: The New Physics for Nonscientists*, ed. riv. San Francisco: Harper & Row.

Zimmer H., edited by J. Campbell. 1946 *Myths and Symbols in Indian Art and Civilization.* Washington

D. C.: Bollingen Foundation Washington, published
Princeton, N.J., by Princeton University Press.

# ESP:
## PARAPSYCHOLOGY AND
## HOLOGRAPHIC REALITY

Extra Sensory Perception (ESP) phenomena provide powerful proof that there is a universe which extends outside our sensorial data. Like Transpersonal Psychology, which deals with what is beyond the I, parapsychology and psi look for connections in the unexplainable. Bruce Greyson, psychiatrist in the Department of the Study of Perception at Virginia University, concentrated on pre-death phenomena (otherwise known as Near Death Experiences) Greyson found in these phenomena a connection with the reawakening of the kundalini.

But ESP, like clairvoyance, OBEs, psycho-kinesis, telekinesis, telepathy and lucid dreams, fits neatly into the frame of the psi of parapsychology of the scientific matrix. I say "scientific" because it is in the universe and meta-universe that ancestral research is conducted to let the archetypal doors of the parallel universes open. All of this is thanks to new holographic hypotheses.

Many anthropologists find a phenomenon similar to the holographic one in mystic consciousness. A hologram is three-dimensional. This 3D game is holographic perception. The mind acts as a receiver, and the hologram is the dimension explored on the perceptive level of the mind. We are in a holographic universe, restricted by our bubble of perception. So we live in morphogenetic fields, as Rupert Sheldrake noticed, and what we classify as an object is nothing more than a screen or perceptive model of interference, interpreted as reality's real data. Our capacity to be selective and our conventions and beliefs fit into consensual reality. We believe, and when we believe we make it conventional.

Parapsychology studies this unidirectional consensus, which is in antithesis to an altered state of consciousness which does not interpret models but perceives them directly. To provide new perceptive models, parapsychology uses itself in psychiatry, but this in turn does not acknowledge ESP, psi and transpersonal phenomena. The Kundalini Syndrome is an example of this, but there are other examples like NDEs and traumas of past lives.

The transpersonal dimension could be a perfect support to psi, because they validate experiential data, concretising the same experience with a solid empirical base. Grof who has used LSD for a long time for his experiments on NOSCs, has re-evaluated Bohm's holographic model, opening it up to his holotropic realms.

It is in this holographic-holotropic binomial that holistic science plays an important role. This is not only because of the undeniable interest that holographic theories have raised but also because of the huge effort Grof has put into the radical revision of the Newtonian-

Cartesian paradigm. Grof who has worked alongside Gregory Bateson, Joseph Campbell, Abe Maslow, Ervin Laszlo, Fritjof Capra, Zina Bennett and Richard Tarnas, supports the paradigm so much so that he has introduced it into the *Psychology of the Future* (Grof , SUNY press 2000).

Grof has collaborated with Campbell in an attempt to find a coherent myth in this new millennium. He has found the myth through his research into the origins of the holotropic man of the future, where science, religion and psychology meet and where the hetero-spatial divide disappears. This is where man is; he has to cross over the threshold into the unknown. This is the threshold of the universe, the threshold of ESP.

# THE HOLOGRAPHIC MIND: HOLOGRAPHIC PERCEPTION IN PSYCHOTIC STATES

What I am about to discuss requires careful analysis; intuitive as well as meta-rational analysis.

Let us first focus on the complicated tapestry called consciousness. The universe, the whole Akashic field of the mind (see Ervin Laslo. 1987. "Akashic field, 'psi field' hypothesis.". *IS Journal* 4-13-28) is an interconnected network of inte-referential events. (See also Karl Pribram's holographic model of the brain,,K. H. Pribram 1971.)

What consciousness sees as a *unicum,* or a unit, can likewise be glimpsed as a break up or separation. The term schizophrenia means "split or separate". In other words, what mystics perceive as unity, Brahman, or a synthesis of the whole universe, is for a schizophrenic a fragmentation of parts; a division.

Here the holographic process enters into play. Since it has been discovered that the holography of the brain has, like schizophrenia and psychosis, the togetherness of subclasses—a kind of space-time continuum in holographic terms—psychotics live in a universe with a holographic quality. However, instead of being made up of mystical experiences, they also tend to separate things compulsively in a failing auto-compulsive attempt to bring back their "sacred-unity."

According to the theory of the implicate order of Bohm's, psychotics and schizophrenics respond to the implicit category of reality, in other words, they respond to the implicate order. This is an order hidden from view which facilitates the connection with an invisible, sub-quantum universe, a deeper order of existence which underlies the illusion of our daily perception.

The universe is cosmic game, a unified network of events in the multi-dimensional field of consciousness. What mystics see as a unitary field is "Lila" (the Hindu's Cosmic Game). Even a psychotic glimpses this connection but he dissociates it and tends to separate and fragment it. His intention is noble, but the modality of drawing near to the implicate order of things is distorted.

Jung stated that psychotics observe a world which is theirs, rich in primordial images. Their universe has an imaginal quality which Jung calls "numinous." But their access to *numinosum* is transitory and temporary and is subject to intermittent flashes. Psychotics, even if they access the rich material of the unconscious, probably do not manage to integrate it into their consciousness. Thus they are dissociated from the primordial material of the collective unconscious.

This collective layer is the place of gods and pathologies. It is the magic place of the mandala. A mandala is a highly liminal experience which like a hologram reveals a way into a parallel reality. A schizophrenic glimpses this reality, but cannot manage to navigate it, or in other words he cannot manage to move from one field to another without his compulsive selectivity being interrupted and no longer controlled.

Compulsive control is similar to a primitive ritual for driving away occult presences which threaten the psyche's mandala: the enclosoure is moved from its sacredness. This attempt at selfpreservation is an effort to preserve the sacred enclosure, the throne of divinity. A schizophrenic perceives life interwoven with divine symbols, but he sees fragments since he cannot manage to see the whole thing. The archetypal presence of the mandala is perceived as a dualistic experience. The enclosure becomes a prison.

But holographically speaking, our world is an illusionary bubble of perception. As the transpersonal philosopher Richard Tarnas (see *Cosmos and Psyche*) suggests, we are no different from schizophrenics with our compulsive tendency to "desacralise." Progress and post-modernity are belittling nature and the cosmos. The mentally ill, as we define them, attempt to restore this cosmos even if they use "primitive" means which are antithetical to consensual reality. Their intention, however, is to sacralise nature, their mind is primitive in the sense that it is mythical. Their perception is primogenious and authentic. Maybe man has one more responsibility when faced with such advanced forms of consciousness and mythical intelligence. An intelligence capable of animating the primordial universe of images, capable of meeting archetypes and mythological motifs of the unconscious.

*Diego Pignatelli Spinazzola*

These structures are primitive in the sense of "archaic" and "liminal." They inhabit "confines"—we call them borderline, paranoid, schizophrenic, psychotic, obsessive and mad; trusting in consensual appearances. However, they are able to permeate the cosmos. What post-modern man has shattered, they put back together, they restore to their sacredness. They perceive the universe as a togetherness of multiple sub-classes. The universe is a "multiplex" to use one of Ken Wilber's terms.[3] But post-modern culture has downgraded these phenomena by referring to them as anomalies. Is it or is it not an anomaly to desacralise nature and the universe? The myth of progress has shown a gradual decline. (See Richard Tarnas.[4]) If there is a fault, it is that these anomalies are permeable: they sing of the sound of the cosmos, whilst post-modern man dulls this sound.

We have scarcely evolved enough to talk about it in Jungian terms, but we presume to dominate the evolved forms of the universe. If we observe the hologram and its parts or components, we notice that they are patterns of information about the whole hologram. Even if they are fragmented, these splinters can be re-arranged to make the whole hologram. We live in a cosmic warehouse, but we draw from a single reservoir, from a single reserve of information. To use one of David Bohm's ideas, each tiny, microscopic part of the holographic plate contains the complete image of the super-hologram.

Finally, in the words of Michael Talbot: *"Our brains mathematically construct an objective reality by interpreting frequencies which are basically projections from another dimension, from a deeper order of existence which is beyond space and time."* (Talbot 1991).

[3]Wilber, K, J. Engler, D. P. Brown. *The Transformation of Consciousness, conventional and contemplative perspective on development.* Boston and London: Shambhala.

[4]Tarnas, R. 2006. *Cosmos and Psyche: Intimations of a New World View.* Viking Press, Penguin Group

## References

Bohm, D. *The holographic paradigm.* Boulder, CO: Shambhala.

Ullman, M. 1986. "Psi and psychopathology.".Society for Psychical Research.

Pribram, K. H. 1971. *Languages of the brain: Experimental paradoxes and principles in neuropsychology.* Englewood Cliffs, N.J.: Prentice-Hall.

———. 1991.*Brain and perception: Holonomy and structure in figural processing.* Hillsdale, N.J.: Lawrence Erlbaum Associates.

Laszlo, E. 1987. The psi-field hypothesis. *IS Journal, 4,* 13-28.

———.1993. *The creative cosmos: A unified science of matter, life, and mind.* Edinburgh: Floris.

———. 1997. *The whispering pond.* New York: Harper Collins.

———. 2001, Sept. 1. Human evolution in the third millennium. *Futures,* 1-11.

———. 2004. *Science and the Akashic field: An integral theory of everything.* Rochester, NY: Inner Traditions.

# MYTHOLOGEMS:
# THE PORTALS OF THE
# UNCONSCIOUS

Where consciousness and unconscious collaborate we find a synthesis, another reintegrated binominal from these two spheres. The cooperation of the binomial conscious/unconscious opens up new perspectives, portals of sacred and mythological spaces and archetypal mythologems.

This perspective is a widening of a sacred door or sanctuary depicted in the Jungian *rotundum*, the so-called *mandala,* which is a sacred enclosed space for Buddhists and Hindus. Where there is collaboration there is at last an alchemic union, a *coniunctio,* also known as a mystic wedding. The synthesis of an alchemic union is, following Jung's classic description, the complement between *Anima* and *Animus*. While the happening of primordial unconscious or indeed the collective unconscious, agents and autonomous models which govern psychic life, archaic motifs denominated archetypes, their flow in the drama of the psyche represents their invasion of the psychic sphere.

In the unconscious region, we again find mythologems which belong to a primordial layer of collective identity. There is a layer which finds itself in states of amplified perception, magical rituals of primitives, witches and shamans. In this layer the intermediate dimension dwells; bridges between the kingdom of the living and the dead, the forebears of ancestral humanity. Here is the bridge of the gods, with whom the shaman is the spiritual mediator, poured into the sacred enclosed space or mandala. The *coniunctio* in fact shows up in the *rotundum* (the symbol of a numinous experience), it is a mandala with eight petals depicting Shiva Srikantha, directed with his pity in four directions or spatial regions. The mandala is a *mundus*, a centre of psychic totality in which the so-called centre expands until it irradiates. A meditator must proclaim the texts of Mahasuka, an infinity of rays which expand in the four cardinal points of cosmic space. Star Gates are four-part patterns which also lie beneath the sacred doors projected in the four directions of space. A connection with the four cardinal points can be found both in Jung's mandala and in Zimmer's two-dimensional Yantra.

Even the Indian swastika is a symbol which indicates the four cardinal points or the Axis Mundi of the universe. In cosmogonies, mythologems hide from this axis mundi as in the Hindu myth of Brahman, or in the Hindu-Buddhist pillars of Ashoka, the first Indian king who was also the patron and disseminator of Buddhism. The cosmic axis is a mythologem which goes back to the origins of unconscious, to the primeval, mythical and archaic era which revealed the divine struggle between light and darkness. In the Vedic myth, Indra fights and defeats the shadowy forces of complex and broken Vritra, who risks threatening and obscuring the universe in a regressive, primordial and shapeless tendency. From this example, one resorts to the significance of analytical psychology, where unconscious is the broken and dispersive force that risks threatening the myth, or to put it better: the conative tension which takes place with the cosmogonic god Indra. But the same tension is used to resolve opposites which the two regions of consciousness and unconscious flee from the complementary binominal in the process of union and total synthesis. Liberation comes from this harmonious synthesis; liberation from the assertive forces of unconscious which are often destructive. In the mandala this unifying synthesis (called *Selbst* by Jung) takes place. In other words, it is individuation process.

Becoming aware of individuation is a state of transcending the usual limitations of the self. This leads to an inter-planetary, cosmic, compassionate and transpersonal feeling. It wakes consciousness up to the design of entire humanity and a jovial return to life. Here the conscious and unconscious binominal opens up to a cosmic and mythologemic vision and the great mystery of existence.

## References

Jung C. G., Karol Kerényi. 1949. *Essays on a Science of Mythology.* Bollingen Series XXII. New York: Pantheon Books ,

———. *Collected Works.* Princeton N.J.: Princeton University Press, and London: Routledge and Kegan Paul LTD.

————. 1956. *Symbols of Transformation.* Collected Works, vol. 5, Bollingen Series XX, Princeton, N.J.: Princeton University Press.

————. 1959. *The Archetypes and the Collective Unconscious.* Collected Works, vol. 9,1. Bollingen Series XX, Princeton, N. J.: Princeton University Press.

————. 1960. *A Review of the Complex Theory.* Collected Works, vol. 8, Bollingen Series XX. Princeton: Princeton University Press.

Zimmer, H., edited by J. Campbell. 1946. *Myths and Symbols in Indian Art and Civilization.* Bollingen Foundation Washington D.C., Published by Princeton University Press, Princeton, New Jersey.

# APPENDIX
# A NEW COSMOGONY

What follows is a cosmogonic fable of beginnings. One of my many interpretations. Nothing is proven or documented from a historical or philological point of view. All I ask is that you link it together as a tale, nothing more.

In the beginning there was a nucleus, a matrix of all archetypes and all universes, images and perceptions. It was like a spider – a unique centre in the cosmic spider's web. Just like a huge spider it intertwined its threads projecting and reabsorbing them in a concentric circle (Bhradaranyaka Upanishad). The universe was the loom of its games. But from this nucleus, the universes continued to proliferate. The hiding place of the spider drew consciousness from its archetypes, eidetic images that Jung called Archetypes of the Collective Unconscious.

Then this spider played in the unconscious and wove symbolic and archetypal threads. This spider is the bindu point in Hindu cosmogony. It is the primordial absolute, the nucleus which opens up for cosmic eras and eons releasing the unobvious and expanding the tangible. This spider is the Absolute which radiates energy and dissolves the whole of the circumference of the spider's web. In this zero dimension, energy cannot be contracted or condensed, so it expands. In a pattern of introjections and extroversions, the spider weaves in this cosmic configuration which, like a two-dimensional Yantra (a concentric configuration) expands and retracts. From the centre of the Yantra, the lines of strength irradiate outwards in concentric circles and dissolve the entire external circumference. The heart of this pulse is the magic polarised by the divine, cosmogonic creation.

The spider wove and enriched its threads. But then one day, at the age of dawn, the florid cities of gold hardened, the ancient dynasties fought to usurp its place, and the archetype of the sacred was preserved and then outclassed by a new civilisation. The splendour of Indra's palaces, whose sky reflected the pearly receptacle, moved away from the solid surfaces of disasters eclipsed by the sun. Surya, the sun-god, distanced himself from the ascetics and the clairvoyants. These same ascetics prayed to Indra to free Surya from the cosmic waters which were trapped by the monstrous Vritra (the demon nicknamed Asura) threatened by a total eclipse. Indra freed the sun from the muddle of celestial waters (*svaratih*) and let them flow back thus completing the cosmogonic myth narrated in the Rg Veda. But the civilisations to come darkened and the gods did not last for long. The fluid centre of the cosmos atrophied and a new era came into being, that of Kali yuga.

Kali, the ferocious and jealous goddess of time, killed and substituted the cosmic spider and from her uterus projected a triangular matrix which the whole universe fell victim to. Starving and never satisfied, Kali devoured transmigrating souls. With shears and a necklace of skulls around her neck and at her sides, she waved around in the path of the blood-red lagoon, severing sentient and non-sentient beings' contact with life.

Just as a praying mantis devours her male, Kali danced on the consort Shiva, she sliced the emanating cosmic illusion with her horrifying look.

Kali was the spider and time was a slave to her service. Once Kali had been the belle of three worlds which Shiva had taken a fancy to, even if the gods and demons argued about the young girl because of her beauty. But Kali together with her tendency stood out more because of her ambivalence her beauty.

Kali yuga takes its name from Black Kali and depicts a black apocalyptic age which had regressed with moral and spiritual disorder, where the cosmos no longer breathed from within the temporal coils of the goddess. The gods paled at the sovereign meddling of the goddess of the universe.

The world, the planet of men, is in danger because of environmental, climactic, ecological and spiritual disasters. If everything returns to original Chaos, only re-absorption by Brahman can put an end to Kali's tyranny. Because of entropy we are moving away from galaxies, and like a bubble of perception we will explode in a new big bang. Kali's reign has brought wars, famine and nationalism to people and religions.

It is not over yet because an avatar called Kalki will come down as the last incarnation of Vishnu (the universal patron god of gods) and he will have to fight the tyrannical empress of the universe. The future saviour, the last cosmic avatar, galloping on a baneful white horse will face the demonic Kali. And a new era will begin again, it will be the noeitic era of victory. The era of knowledge of the forces of illusion held in check by an ephemeral sovereign.

# TANTRA:
# THE MYSTIC OF THE
# UNIVERSE

The Tantras, sacred verses of Shivaite denomination, stand as a symbol of the universe. An actual mysticism such as Sufism and the Kabballah, the Tantras offer a synthetic and metaphysical outlook of the cosmos. They are the sacred garment where the one materializes in the All and unfolds phonematically in many shapes. Shiva above all is the god who works the synthesis in its five operations of emission, duty, re-absorption, obfuscation and destruction. By sending forth the phonemes, he reabsorbs them in himself and in the plans of consciousness. The superior phonematic syllable sabda-varna (The sounds are the essence of the mantras. All sounds are the essence of Shiva Ishvarapratyabijnahrdaya).

"A" is the vocal from whose unfolding a dualistic distinction between subject and object. "A" is privileged in the sound "AUM" (from A, the Unity, to the multifaceted Aum). Conversely, the reabsorbing (samhara) is from the multifaceted "M" to the One. "A"; for example "MAHA", the process of reiteration and AHam = emission, projection. MAHA symbolizes the ethical order of the universe which returns in itself. The Aham, that is, the I, is the supreme mantra. It is the I the maker of the cosmic process celebrated in Shiva, the paramatman who does not intercede the universe because he rules it as pure consciousness (cit) and as the cosmic matrix from which all forms come into being in categories (*tattvas*), self-reflecting in Shiva's pulsing heart. But consciousness may also contract and take the shape of the multifaceted *idam* in the presence of the divine potencies (*shakti*), who hypnotize the *Aham*. It is the *Aham* who plays the lead in the cosmic scene. Etymologically, Aham is made of the "A" of *anuttara*, which symbolizes the unity-order of the cosmos, the One which transcends the All in the universe before the multifaceted unfolding which culminates in the "M" of "multitude."

It may happen that the aham, the undistinguished consciousness, may be dazzled by the many colours of the Idam, unaware that it is reflecting in one of its projections (*a-suddhi*). Shiva transcends all projections. He is not touched by the dualizing power of illusion and surpasses the duality of the consciousness hypnotised and bathed in the *idam*.

A human being is not very sensitive to ultra-violet light, which has psychedelic characteristics. A psychotic may mistake it for reality, but within both factors lie the hypnotic power of illusion.

Shiva transcends the dyad of time-space in a tri-dimensional triad which has no boundaries. Sambhu's trident, hypostasis of the Lord, represents the dimensions transcended in non-dual unity (*anuttara*), and while the drum (*damaru*) beats, the floating flow of psychological time, the dance rules in the ecstatic initiation of death, reflection of dancing Shiva (*lila-murti*).

It is in this reflection that the person meditating has to visualize how, in a blazing circle, the transcending of the progressive reabsorbing of the plans of consciousness, purified by the fire of the dance of Shiva Nataraja takes place. Shiva stands as a superior Lord of the Wheel (*chakreshvara*) who as a three-headed being fills the universe (Trisiromata, quoted in Ksemaraja, Ishvarapratyabhijnahrdaya). The three-headed being ambiguously is the contracted consciousness (*citta*) who was bathed in the ocean of duality "so as the Blessed has the universe as a body, so its essence in contraption of the consciousness ("citta", Ishvarapratyabijnahrdaya) ".

This ocean is the residence of the Aham, of the superior self, non compressed, but extended as absolute universal consciousness (*cid-atma*). Even the non initiation reaches Shiva if understood as unique principle (*bindu*) in the act of conscience of universal trascendence. The condition of *Shiva-bhattaraka* transcends all and is made of pure light (*prakasha*); to Shiva belong conditions of the being who are only forms of light (*pratyabijnahrdaya*). But there is also a way called "The way of Sambhu," that is Shiva, a way which is purely noetic which sees Shiva as (*turya*), the fourth state, the one that transcends all. Shiva's freedom is in his five operations. It is because of this game (*lila*) that the I dares with himself in the attempt to overtake, and the self acknowledges himself as the maker of the Universe-All, of the whole cosmic process and of its origin.

## References

Pio Filippani Ronconi: Vak La Parola Primordiale ed. Pungitopo 1987 (ME).

Abhinavagupta, Paratrisika-Vivarana: "the Secret of Tantric Mysticism" by Jaideva Singh, Swami Lakshmanjee, Motilal Banarsidass.

# ARCHETYPES OF
# REVELATION

Life keeps going like a piece of thread interwoven with archetypes which are hidden and then uncover themselves in the meshes of an eternal present. Archetypes are part of a flicker of plans and symbols—intuitions which appear in the dynamic debate about time.

The phenomenon of these symbols, or clues, is the same archetypal nature that takes place amongst the workings of the Divine. Their voice seems to belong to a hidden order. By nature, the self that is thought hides and uncovers itself among the archetypes, and among the phenomena of light, shade, sound and silence.

"Freedom of the self consists as much in the differentiation of what is not differentiated, as in unification, with an interior synthesis, of what is differentiated." (Abhinavagupta, in R. Gnoli, Tantraloka p.28 L.V. I 31). This verse from Abhinavagupta, the greatest Indian philosophical thinker who lived in Kashmir in the 10th and 11th centuries, clarifies every sort of speculation about the dynamic nature of light and thought which is expressed and becomes a phenomenon itself by shaping and re-shaping itself in the mirror of the divine.

"The things that we see around us, and with these and our own interior motions, there are no others, say the shaivaite, if not images (*abhasa*), free manifestations of the force of the self which through these, expresses and affirms itself" (Abhinavagupta., in R. Gnoli, Tantraloka p.28 L.V. I 31).

Irradiation is, for the shaivaite, the same nature as Shiva, it is the light of consciousness, the universal source which has always used the self-revealing manifestation of everything in the noumenic and phenomenal existence of its resplendent arch.

This reality is a projection—a playful manifestation, as the Hindus would say, of the god Shiva. Free thought, which through its cosmic use, through its phenomenal differentiation and occultation and its hiding, believing itself to be other than it is, returns to take hold of consciousness, realising the apparent multiplicity of everything and plunging it into the fullness of the self, free from any dualism. But light-thought, the dynamic synthesis of being, is not only a playground for the gods, it is also a revealing downhill slope for archetypes which are actors on the same stage of human life. They act as revelations or as the *mundus imaginalis,* described so thoroughly by Corbin. The revelation of the symbolic light of Shiva is mirrored in the soul, or the *animus.*

"Prakasha-vimarsha is actually the first vibration of light. In this first creative vibration, which ploughs through the quiet sea of consciousness, pre-exists the whole multiplicity" as Somananda said. Since the freedom of self means differentiating oneself from various others, research or its conation tries hard to resolve the opposites in a *coniunctio oppositorum* of divine reflections. In this conation (which is a synthesis of a perpetual dynamism) the directed way to the divine takes place. The divine is the seat of an undifferentiated link where One becomes many and many becomes One again.

# NUMINOUS:
# THE ALTAR OF THE SACRED

The plans of ascension are the configuration of that invisible that reveals the sacred nature in numinous. Only when the veil of the numinous is discovered does the sacred show itself in all its plentifullness. Like an altar strewn with incenses and relics, it adorns itself with pulsating magic that is veiling this sacrosanct mystery. The numinous is ecstasy with the divine. The numinous happens through the perception of the invisible, where the world of the invisible opens itself it looms. This perception is the entry amidst the altars of the sacred.

The sufis use the image of the mystic Kabah, the holy black stone, the Hindus use the image of the Ishvara-mantra, the Buddhists that of the mandala, the Taoists use the image of the flying dragons. The urgency of the sacred is a mystical truth for the researchers of the truth.

The mantra is like a mystical syllable that permeates the cosmic universe of the Hindu where the tantras are revealing the arcane. The Shaivite symbol has emerged in the holy temples of India, at the residence of the cosmic mountain, the centre of the antique worshipping (*kula*) of God and the Goddess (*akula*).

Shiva is the awakening of the supreme enlightenment, the symbol of the consciousness that ultimately has won against illusion, the veiling made by maya. The sacred wants to go out through the door of sanctuary.The ceremonies and the rites of initiation made throught baths in ashes are the urgency of the transfigured likeliness of palingenesis, and a revulsion to all levels of consciousness. Shiva is the consciousness that awakens itself throught the consciousness in the consciousness where the divine lets the sacred shine.

Sacred like a relic, like a deciphering of the devanagari of sanskrit, sacred like the Ganges.

Sacred like the bull of Shiva, Nandi, sacred like the Goddess Kali with her countless arms, customizing time.

The numinous pulses in the symbol of magical archetypes, of the sacred in all levels of Being, and the supreme ascension, transcends, immanent yet enfolds the numinous. The numinous of the sacred essence shedding like a piece of Indian incense or like the arabesque of a cathedral.

The numinous is like sacred contemplation, like a platonic vision, like the motor of the sky-blue sphere of Aristotle, like the hierarchy of the angels, the cherubs and the celestial intelligences. The Sacred and the pulsating of this numinous is living in God, where time and space ends, and in a single moment in life man can perceive up to a certain point this revealing of the veiled Being in the Being, where all times and all places are flowing into one and unique moment, where his time ends and where the arcane was initiated.

# COSMIC WATERS IN THE COSMOGONIC DIMENSION

Water is the cosmogonic dimension in which the self, by involutionary immersion, sinks into the abysses. So, in antithesis to a super-spiritual, evolutionary consideration so well sung about in Rig Veda, we can pass over the myth as a late puranic in the immersion of cosmic waters (*svaratih*), in search of, not in the discovery of, celestial light (*svar*).

Water is the purifying rhythm of life, but immersion in the cosmic balm is divine revelation, it is the seat of immortality. The myth of Indra goes back to immersion, co-agitation and the search for fulfilment through Brahman and supreme prayer. Dhiti, the clairvoyant's vision, is a subterranean immersion of consciousness in the watery and vaporous sub-conscious.

Water is not an ambivalent dimension, but the playground for ambivalences or better still, the base on which the myths fight each other like children of a cosmic night. Clairvoyants used *dhiti* to open up visions, and they penetrated the vaporous tunnels where celestial lights were trapped. If sinking immersion is the first phase, revelation of light is the second, the search which culminates in illumination through a cosmogonic effort in an attempt to free the obstruction which veils the light. The cosmogonic warrior called up by the Rishi, the Veda clairvoyants, is Indra, and light is Indra's reward. Indra is the outer layer who modelled existence from non-existence and created paths through the darkness with the help of the sun.

But the gigantic obstruction, the primordial monster Asura Vrtra, the dark obscurer, pervaded primeval chaos with unknown forces in a primordial universe. Chaos and confusion could not co-exist, so Indra struck Vritra down with his thunderbolt. Vrtra was the chaotic, broken force which held the Sun's hidden energy in the clothes of Surya and Savitr, who were also children of the waters.

And if the Suns hide from the waters, the mystical vision of "dhi" *is* water, a matrix of their creations. From this, water cosmogony takes place and from the search for the divine situated in the abysses of an ancestral sub-conscious, re-emerges in the awareness of celestial light. It almost sounds like a fable, but it is not. Water is the myth of creation by whose powers Indra created the earthly and dual world and led it away from the undifferentiated, broken complex; a regressive cycle which is repeated in the "Creation at the hands of the Wild Boar," in the myth of Vishnu the victor over Ananta, the gigantic serpent which threatened the universe between its coils.

Cosmic waters are at the base of this primordial event. Vishnu, god of life, sleeps above the clairvoyants, caressed by his wife Sri Lakshmi, in the waters which run into a state of suspension (*moha*) between the disappearance of one universe and the birth of another.

Waters also have a purifying nature, like the bathing ritual in the Ganges, the sacred river in which it is said that every Hindu can be reborn into one of Vishnu's paradises, Vaikuntha or as a servant in the domain of Shiva; in other words beside these gods. Offering up a prayer with sanctified water (*argha*) is among the rites of Brahman initiation (*diksha*). The act of immersion and bathing in the Ganges takes up the cosmogonic principle that the cosmic waters are the divine flow of cosmogonic events.

Prayers of adoration with flowers of incense, bathing and linga constitute the Shaivite image of immersion—from immanence to transcendence, from idam to divine ipseity. Ashuddi is dispersion into idam, into multiplicity, while shudda is immersion of the self in awareness, in the heart of Shiva (*Hridaya*).

Between these two operations of Shiva, water is the receptacle of awareness in the state of immersion of the self as a re-appropriation of a cosmogonic dimension. Water is in favour of such a dimension (and is favourable). The Sanskrit characters devanagari were seen as notable in water and from them the meditators and devoted recited mantras, carried out dhiti and visualisations.

Water is a symbol of transformation; it is the border between parallel worlds. The myth of creation tells of a gigantic cosmic egg covered in primordial waters of the universe. The lotus symbolises water's exit from darkness, but it is also a mythical-cosmogonic symbol of the creation of the gods and cosmic centre like mount Meru where devas lived. Brahma, the god of gods who appeared from Vishnu's belly button, sleeps in primordial waters to give life to a new creation. Maintaining the waters in their dispersion and involution puts forward again the course of life and myth. The myth of creation. Water is also a vehicle of descent for the cosmic avatar, as it is the border between the earthly and ultra-earthly world, between the sensitive and super-sensitive world. Water is the kingdom of the amphibious male naga and the nagini female snakes, as well as princesses who live in the deep waters, and the makara, aquatic dragons represented by sculptures on Hindu torana.

The makara is an aquatic monster generated by waters to fight the Sura divinities and to threaten cosmic order (*rita*) which gods like Indra and Agni obey. The makara, to use a more appropriate adjective, are anthropomorphic creatures, once they were devas, celestial divinities, but they became demons (*asura*). Consanguinity links Asura and the gods (*Sura*) and this is repeated in the myth of Veda. A struggle between children of the night and children of light swimming in the bottom of the cosmic abyss where the waters are creation and resurrection, absorption and catharsis, vision and exaltation.

# THE KOSMOGONICAL
# MANDALA

The human being is a manifestation of the god (Ishwara). The Ishwara is an extension of the human being.

These statements point to very precise facts, and they are real for whoever has recognized the archetypal dimension of his own Self; they are real because they not only give the foundations for a "religious attitude" but also the assumptions for a metaphysical one. The "metaphysical attitude" meets the "religious attitude" on a higher level, therefore forming the transpersonal dimension.

The Ishwara-deity is an extension generated by the psychic powers of man and the more symbolic representation of a psychological mandala. Once upon a time, man dwelt in the symbol which opened up in images projected in the mandala, the home of a symbiotic archetypal/ecstatic unity with the god (Ishwara). The primeval archaic man was in touch with mythical perception filled with symbolism. But the symbol was the more direct manifestation of an intimate relationship with the divinity; man lived with the gods (deva) and shared their heavenly palaces (Realms of the Brahma). The mystical union with the divine vibrated with light and magic in the archaic man. The physical moved in the meta-physical to reach the psychical; the three worlds: physical, metaphysical and psychical coexisted in harmony.The tendency of man to overcome himself, to extend beyond the limit of the body is a stage which may be found even in childhood. Children possess their own well-built mandala; within them the representation of the psychic mandala is revived by the high density images for the television.

This is why the cartoons are necessary to children, they return to the child the colours of a sharp experience with the mandala. The cartoons give the key to a cosmos where only children may access. We may say that children constantly recognize their mandalic scheme; the only disadvantage is that they are not aware of it. The child, moreover, doesn't stop the emotions of the changeable flow of the perceptions; on the contrary he enriches them within his mandalic Cosmos. Cartoon, robots, anime Geeg-Manga, they all crowd the cosmos of the child, they are his myths. The child can't legitimize his partaking in such experiences, even though that universe is very close to him. Like a clay wheel which still turns, in the child there are also prefigured schemes of experiences. The metaphysical experience is felt as extra-corporeal, which is out of the body. There is no sharp separation, but rather an extension. Every fantasy of the child is an extension outside of the body. This experience is outside of all conceptual schemes, is an experience with the divine. Such an experience, which I'd call a metaphysical experience, is already within the child and uses the meta-psychic element. In any case it is always the Ishvara which reaches out, either to the child or to the adult, only the latter cannot find the rush to extend on those levels, and thus holds back to a dualistic level.

As a matter of fact, the child is endowed with sensitivity and is able to build a bridge with the Ishwara, visiting his astral dimension, utilising his psychic extension, while in the adult the opposite perception is triggered as that very same dimension has become a self-circumscription.

Man, instead of extending in the outside, projects inside. He's the apex of dualism under a false perception. Just so, that which man calls the real world is nothing other than actions of internal introjections. The cosmic extension becomes a cosmic illusion and all the game ends in the hands of the opponent, Maya.

The intact scheme undergoes a transformation in the evolution of facts and all thecomponents which constituted the composite mandala fall apart; it effects a fragmentation of the mandalic scheme, and man loses his bearings. All becomes blurred chaos and fragmentation. The Self doesn't recognize himself in the total design of things, but rather sees himself as a temporary guest in a stranger universe. Moreover, those elements which were familiar to him as a child move away. Man not only walked away from "the house of the gods" but is no longer even able to recognize it. Even if the gods are benevolent toward him, the human being snubs their attentions, identifying himself with the shallow scheme of things, discarding *a priori* the residence of his archetype. We may say that if as children we hold hands with the gods, once we grow up they deny it to us. But this emancipation of man from the divine is nothing but a conventional hypostasis and an escape from the sacred.

But if the sacred was the place where man dwelt with the divine beings, now the concept is the home of the human. It was the concept which threw him out of the kingdom of the gods to hand him to the terrible mother illusion. Now the concept has divided them until when they will reabsorbed in the divine game of the Brahman (the Demiurge).Visnu, the warrior-god, a creature born out of the early chaos, and Shiva, the god who had to drink ambrosia of the gods, are the main figures in the Hindu pantheon, not because they are ambivalent and anthropomorphic, but because one represents the cosmic reintegration, the other its dissolution. In the aesthetic expression of the Trimurti, it is the Brahman, traditionally represented in the androgynous Prajapati, who sits between these two deities: Vishnu and Shiva. And if Indra set free the early waters imprisoned by Vtra, letting them flow freely, in Shiva the impermanent continuum is interrupted by his dance of maya (tandava) in the circle of fire of the cosmic dissolution.

The idea of the *tremendum* is in Shiva, the multi-faceted, ambivalent dimension. Shiva is feared even by his most fervent devotee because he knows that the god sends forth the illusion, holding it up with his strength (*shakti*) and like in a game of cosmic dice misleads the world projecting the Maya, until he become tired and dissolves it in the souls of the believer.

That is why Shiva, even if feared as an exasperation of the universe, he is also the promise of a final redemption; for he, manifesting in the luminous extension (Shiva-tattva) of the man/Ishwara, frees from the dualistic dimension the non-awake being that is relegated in the dark medium of Maya in an eternal samsara.

In the Ishwara we find the non-dual principle as all the manifest is a condensation of Shiva at the actual state, and to him returns under dual form, to dissolve again in the formless non-duality. Here is the mandala.

The actual world is only the illusion of an invisible law, from which man has separated through objectivation and individuation (*anava*) without realizing that what he values is only mere illusion as Indra's net.

So we haven't accepted the ambrosia of the gods, the non-dualistic kingdom which the gods offered us. It is easy to understand how the human drama is all a fight between word and symbol, dualism and non-dualism, between concept and image. In the dualistic path which is personal growth, man strips the symbol through a dichotomizing objectivation, maturing the dualism between the I and the surroundings, between subject and object.

The dualism of subject/object open the way to metaphysical dualism and psychological dualism. Even if in the child these elements are not present, society and the education system do all they can to introduce them, so that those dualistic remains will give the premises for the metaphysical dualism. This particular dualism is the circumscription of space/time. Such a thing is unnatural for the child, as he feels the extension as an extension of his own being, while Man, on the other hand, gets used to this dualism, turning it into a "constant law," constant as the feeling of being a stranger to a world which does not belongs to us. All multiplicity is a strange manifestation for the dualistic being. Metaphysical dualism is the incapability to see the invisible which fills the space, this invisible rules from above as metaphysical, archetypal law. The invisible (Akshara) rules each given inner attitude and is also an Ishwara in itself.

It is up to the perception to sense the awareness of the invisible. "It doesn't live in a remote imaginary, but is potentially enclosed to the stage of wakefulness in several forms of consciousness separated by subtle screens. We may spend our lives without even suspecting their existence, but it suffices to apply a certain stimuli that with a light touch they will reveal themselves fully" (William James, my own re-translation). Each perception weaves the mandala with colours and diagrams, where man recognizes himself at the centre of the universe, in that Axis Mundi resurrected from chaos, where Indra reabsorbed it in the early principle, taking it back form the one to the many, and from the many to the one, to the still light of the awakened consciousness. In such contest, the waters are cosmogonical because they are the subconscious flow of a hypothetical inner journey, in the descent of the being in the realm of the Ishwara.

# On the Thresholds of the Transpersonal Psychology: A Science beyond the Boundaries

David Bohm, an excellent example of a mystic, besides being a scientific researcher and father of the "holographic paradigm," theorised a non-manifest (implicate order), that is subject to an unveiled (explicate order) of which our world is part. The holographic journeys have stimulated the discoveries of Stanislav Grof's holotropic realms of unconscious. These are journeys, which explore nonordinary states of consciousness (NOSC) and confer a holistic and transpersonal vision of the universe. The hologram has within itself the human brain, a kind of holographic plaque, which explores its configurative dynamics. We are cast in a Holographic Universe and wrapped in a bubble of perception called "the world."

But the hologram explores lucid dreams, the near-death experiences, NDE, and the Out-of-the-Body

Experiences OBEs, the journeys into the cosmos away from the connection with the body. As Grof noted, "man is an extension of the whole, and can get experiential access to the whole cosmic network" (Grof 1988). Bohm also revealed this, the man-entity, extension of a universe which Bohm saw as holographic and Grof as holotropic state of consciousness.

In mystical terms, Transpersonal Psychology offers a wide range of themes. Mysticism, as a theoretical and philosophical matrix besides than an experiential one, represents the fulcrum of transpersonal studies. These studies go beyond the orthodoxy of science, because Transpersonal Psychology appears as a non-aprioristic science, as Jung would maintain. That is, it explores states and dimensions which are excluded *a priori* from all that which lays the basis of rationality and empirical data. But it was William James, his father, who laid the basis for mystical and transpersonal studies. The Transpersonal Psychology is science beyond boundaries and is not to be discredited by the framework of mainstream psychology. Abraham Maslow opened the doors to such teaching, calling it trans-humanistic, that is, beyond the irrational, socio-centric and cognitive-centric states, widely used by psychology.

The new Fourth Force explored dimensions which had to deal with a phenomenology of the higher sensible. The experiences of cosmic consciousness, altered states of consciousness, and unions with the sacred, would become frontiers for this new science; frontiers beyond the mind. The transpersonal had to deal with such frontiers as a gnoseologic, noumenic theoretic; an immanence in the transcendent or, vice versa, transcendence in the immanent. The transpersonal featured both esoteric elements taken from eastern cultures and religions: from Buddhism, Taoism and from Shaivism; this last current, for example, accepted the state of supreme awareness above the noumenic data, of the perceptible, the visible; that is as pure objectivation of the cosmic consciousness itself, Shiva.

So the sacred eastern temples multiplied in the mystical East of transpersonal psychology. The reality announced by seers in Vedic India with the famous phrase: *Tat Tvam Asi,* You Are It, becomes domain and final aim of the psychological destination aimed by the Transpersonal, so emphasising that dimension of man in the ecstasy with the divine, in the ecstasy with the sacred.

William James hypothesized the existence of a thin, supra-sensible veil where lay unfolded all the different forms of awareness separated by the thinnest of screens.

In this thought we find *in nuce* the philosophical concept of *maya*, the veil that separates the forces of the sensible universe from the empirical, rational objectivity. *Maya* is the darkener, the unsurpassable screen that separates us from the last truth, from the last awareness. Because, if all is *maya*, we have to agree that the ultimate reality is situated outside such a screen.

That in this screen are trapped the mind games is an irrational aprioristic element which is not to be underestimated. Transpersonal Psychology considers the thin bind, which exists between man and the universe, and makes it cosmic in yogic terms. The macrocosm as revelation of the microcosm and vice versa lay under the universal elements as awakening points called *chakras*, the wheel which awakens Shiva, called by the Hindus the Divine.

In the transpersonal there is a rich and delicate cosmology which is weaved with arcane echoes and reveals the East, as the West is in the Greek myths. Richard Tarnas is a clever researcher of the Greek arcane, author of *Cosmos and Psyche* (Tarnas 2006), and *The Passion of the Western mind* (Tarnas 1991) a scrupulous and meticulous investigator of the astrological archetypal patterns in with the cosmos is embedded. The transpersonal journeys in Plato's hyperuranium not only gain a transpersonal corpus when meeting astrological influences, but as well as esoteric and archetypal of a mystical East. India is the propitiating source of this encounter under the sign of its myths, of its cosmogonical realities taken from the Vedas and unveiled as archetypes of an extra-rational, transpersonal domain.

This reality and this certainty, which is above history, concretise as hyerophanies and cosmogonies and as unveiling of the sacred, unveiling and revealing. And the revelation is implicit in the origin of the veiling. This stimulates the intuitive mind toward new galaxies, new systems, and new confines to explore and overcome; confines which propose new paradigms, new theorems and new discoveries at the thresholds of the transpersonal.

# CONCLUSION
# STANISLAV GROF AND KEN WILBER'S SPECTRUM MODEL OF PSYCHOLOGY: A TRANSPERSONAL SYNTHESIS

For Maslow and Stanislav Grof, who were the precursors of new theories which integrated old models, the pioneering directions of William James and C. G. Jung opened new avenues in transpersonal and archetypal explorations. They also threw emerging new paradigms into the spotlight.

Transpersonal Theory is the daughter of a declaration of independence, which has regained its *status quo* in front of an empirical science that is deeply rooted in reductionism. Now that the Cartesian vision is obsolete, transpersonal science integrates evolutionary and involutionary theories which find their meta-theoretical scaffolding in Ken Wilber's model of systems. Many transpersonal theorists back away from Wilber's integral post-metaphysical theories, stating clearly why they disagree. Stanislav Grof often considered Wilber's model and used it to complement theoretical work related to his experiential system. Although it is a valid model, it can appear to have some basic structural incoherencies.

Stanislav Grof found Wilber's integral spectrum model of psychopathology to be flawed and where the approach was experiential, he noted a certain deficit regarding the whole transpersonal issue. In other words, Wilber's model presents to the evolution/involution consciousness paradigm from pre-ego and ego to centaur. He also presents an evolution from the centaur phase to the trans-ego and transpersonal phase.

As it is very detailed, Wilber's model is considered by the majority of the community of theorists and transpersonal community. As Wilber's theory is integral, he has remained at some distance from his colleagues. In Wilber's system, which is based essentially on Aurobindo's global spectrum model, there are a series of stages which move towards an evolving spiritual path and a series of etiologies best defined as transpersonal pathologies. In theory, beyond the pre-personal and personal level studied by traditional and dynamic psychology, there is a third level which joins a fourth one: the transpersonal dimension. Ken Wilber imagines these levels as transpersonal fulcrums meaning they go beyond those of the development of the Self, and they are used to reach the Transpersonal Self. They are used spiritually, to define experiences which cannot be described rationally.

The transpersonal includes these three fulcrums: from psychic and subtle to causal. The point at which orthodox psychology stops dealing with the realms of the ego, which culminate in the centaur phase (integration of the self, separation and individuation), is the point where the work of Transpersonal Psychology begins. There is not much of a gap between the ego dimension and the transpersonal dimension, and everything moves towards the centaur or a self which is ready to integrate the resulting transpersonal stages.

So far so good, because transpersonal psychology has shown that it deals with non-inclusive stages, i.e. it is excluded *a priori* from orthodox psychology and from corresponding therapeutic interventions. This third transpersonal level, which also has three other fulcrums, ranging from VII to IX (in Wilber's fulcrum), is an area excluded from traditional and conventional psychology which uses post-biographical models according to the principals represented in the psychology of the self (see Mahler, Kohut and Kernberg.) Wilber is an authority on the incoherence of these models, excluding *a priori* a series of factors and circumstances in the transpersonal dimension,having taken the new transpersonal level into the limelight and into knowledge with the inherent pathologies of Yogis – Saints – Sages. (See Wilber, K., J. Engler, D. P. Brown. 1986. *Transformation of Consciousness: Conventional and Contemplative Perspectives on Development*. Boston and London: Shambhala.)

Wilber also superficially put a spotlight on the transpersonal model with the stages and fulcrum of transition. According to Grof however, Ken Wilber's model, which is inherent in Transpersonal Psychopathology, is flawed when he rejects the perinatal matrices as part of the whole spectrum of pathology. These matrices are part of the whole transpersonal dimension. In these dimensions, the matrices are important experiential cornerstones of the transpersonal model. Grof's biggest criticism of Wilber is that he placed his trust in post-natal theories and in the classic psychology of the self, and that he excludes a series of factors and circumstances which form part of the transpersonal dimension and its experiential field; this is something that Wilber seems to have not considered.

Conventional psychology, which is not familiar with Grof's work, defines the perinatal level of unconscious or basic perinatal matrices (BPMs). The advent of these matrices is important in the transpersonal phase because it indicates intra-uterine dynamics, which return to the antecedent and post-birth stage. These are experiential dynamics which go back to a perinatal biography (and to a process of biological birth which is found in karmic experiences through experiencing previous lives) and this happens again in the experience of nonordinary states of consciousness. Here, at a regressive level, one enters a deep state, at a karmic level, to explore the basic perinatal matrices and their experiential dynamics (COEX = condensed experiences.)

Wilber seems to have excluded these dynamics, which are very important turning points in the transpersonal stage of the experience of death and rebirth. These dynamics appear as integrated parts of the transpersonal dimension. According to Grof, this is where Wilber's model is inconsistent: he lacks the basic presuppositions needed to articulate the whole transpersonal question. Wilber deals with evolution, to be precise an evolutionary/ involutionary cosmogenesis and a global or "integral" spectrum, with on theoretical presuppositions. Yet he lacks basic presuppositions on an experiential level. Not being an explorer in the field as Grof is, Wilber constructed his system on presuppositions that had already been validated and tested by psychology, which deals with the stages of development of the self, i.e. post-biographical experience.

Grof believes that for a more comprehensive spectrum model, we need to consider the BPMs matrices (basic perinatal matrices) and their dynamics. Wilber rejects the sequential hypothesis of the matrices and concentrates instead on the uroboric, pre-ego, ego and centaur phases, affirming that a real transpersonal experience occurs at the mature levels of the ego: from the mature ego to the centaur, from the centaur and subtle, causal realms to Atman.

Grof distances himself from Wilber's theories in favour of experiences which he calls NOSC (non-ordinary states of consciousness). This experiential practice acts as an interface to these BPM matrices, and acts as their corresponding experiential field. While the matrices are theoretical models, NOSC are their experiential counterpart. Still, within Wilber's model, the centaur opens up to the whole transpersonal experiential field, which is an abandonment of the mature ego. However, according to Wilber, it is normal for the transpersonal stages to be excluded in the pre-ego experience. Wilber believes that transpersonal experiences invade the evolved phases of the ego and do not involve experiences which can be found on a pre-ego, or childlike level.

Wilber sees this supposition of the steadfast ego in the centaur phase as a genuine transpersonal phase. For Wilber, the individual regresses into pre-ego phases and is flooded by trans-ego phases, because of the would-be filter and the dysfunction of the egoic syntax. All of this leaves the individual exposed to a "magical and mythical referential thought," just when egoic syntax starts to fail and one's consciousness is flooded with trans-ego material. This leaves the individual unprotected and at risk of psychic inflation.

According to Grof, transpersonal domains also occur in Wilber's so-called pre-immature phase and it is also possible to have transpersonal encounters in the intra-uterine phase. This is the subtle difference between *pre* and *trans*. This experience can be relived though NOSC. In short, Wilber's uroboric pre-phase state is very different than Grof's basic perinatal matrices. Wilber's concept is more the transcendence of a mature ego than a regression into transpersonal realms and a karmic experience of death and rebirth. In Transpersonal Psychology, both Grof's and Wilber's diverse systems manage to complement each other. Wilber's theoretical field opens onto Grof's experiential field, and vice versa. They are the yin and yang of the same structure, the same dynamic field which includes other basic theoretical, experiential, morphogenetic, ontogenetic, archetypal, mythological, philosophical, anthropological, and inter-agent_structures. They are all equally in tune with each other in the large experiential, meta-theoretical field of transpersonal studies.

## FOR AN EXTENSIVE EXAMINATION, SEE ALSO:

*Ken Wilber's spectrum psychology. Observations from Clinical Consciousness Research.,* by Stanislav Grof M.D.

## References

Grof, S. & C. Grof. 2000. *The Stormy Search for The Self.* New York: Perigee Books.

Grof, S. 1975.*Realms of Human Unconscious*. New York: Viking Press.

Grof, S. & C. Grof. 1980. *Beyond Death*. London: Thames and Hudson.

Grof, S. 1988. *The Adventure of Self Discovery*. Albany, N.Y: State University New York Press.

Grof, S. & C. Grof C. 1989. "Spiritual Emergency: When Personal Transformation becomes a Crisis," New Consciousness Reader. Los Angeles: J. P. Tarcher.

Grof, S. 1975. *Realms of the Human Unconscious: Observations from LSD Research*. New York: Viking Press.

——— 1980. *LSD Psychotherapy*. Pomona, CA: Hunter House.

——— 1985. *Beyond the Brain: Birth, Death, and Transcendence in Psychotherapy*. Albany, N.Y: State University New York Press.

———. 1988. *The Adventure of Self-Discovery*. Albany, N.Y.: State University New York Press

Grof , S., Zina Bennett. 1992. *The Holotropic Mind*. San Francisco: Harper Collins MAPS. 1992

Grof, S. 1998. *The Cosmic Game: Exploration of the Frontiers of Human Consciousness*. Albany, N.Y: State University New York Press.

———. 2000. *Psychology of the Future. Lesson from Modern Consciousness Research*. Albany, N.Y: State University New York Press.

Grof S. & C. Grof. 2000. *The Stormy Search for the Self.* New York: Perigee/Tarcher and Los Angeles: Putnam.

Jung, C. G. 1956. *Symbols of Transformation.* Collected Works, vol. 5, Bollingen Series XX, Princeton, N.J.: Princeton University Press.

―――. 1959. *The Archetypes and the Collective Unconscious.* Collected Works, vol. 9,1. Bollingen Series XX, Princeton, N. J.: Princeton University Press.

―――. 1960. *A Review of the Complex Theory.* Collected Works, vol. 8, Bollingen Series XX. Princeton: Princeton University Press.

Tarnas R. 2006. *Cosmos and Psyche: Intimations of a New World View.* Penguin Group.

Teun Goudriaan and Sanjugupta. 1981. *Hindu Tantric and Sakta Literature.* Wiesbaden.

Wilber K. 1977. *The Spectrum of Consciousness.* Wheaton, Ill.: Quest.

―――. 1981. *Up from Heden.* New York: Doubleday/ Anchor.

―――. 1982. *A Social God.* New York: McGraw-Hill.

―――. 1982. *The Holographic Paradigm and Other Paradoxes.* Boston: Shambhala.

Wilber K., J. Engler, D. P. Brown. 1986. *The Transformation of Consciousness, Conventional and ContemplativePperspective on Development.* Boston and London: Shambhala.

Wilber K. 2000. *A Brief History of Everything.* Shambhala.

———. 2000. *Integral Psychology.* Shambhala.

# GROF-IAN GLOSSARY: BPMS AND COEXS

1. The BPMs (basic perinatal matrices) and
2. COEX (systems of condensed experiences)

## BASIC PERINATAL MATRICES

BPM: These are general experiential patterns related to the stages of biological birth. These BPM are used here as a theoretical model, and do not necessarily imply causal nexus.

COEX: Systems of Condensed Experience.

A COEX system is a specific memory constellation comprised of a condensed form of experiences (and/or fantasies) from different life periods of the individual. Memories belonging to a particular COEX system have a similar basic theme or contain similar elements and are accompanied by a strong emotional charge of the same quality. It should be understood that the

COEX systems are generally sub-ordinate to the BPMs, but they show a great degree of relative functional independence.

# Divine Madness: Unveiling the Myth of Psychosis

## Reliving of the Ancient Soul of the Ancestors

Does madness exist? I don't think so. In other words we are speaking about the complexity of the human psyche. What people call madness is a gateway to the numinous. Mad people are possessed by gods; they are the repositories of ancient truths and promethean beings that are able to access the numinous as well as to connect with the superpersonal and supernatural forces of the unconscious. Madness does not really exist except within the narrow medical DSM and ICP framework as arbitrary and inadequated categoryies used as a way of explaining the rich and extraordinary complexity of the human psyche that lies at the threshold of consciousness and is not protected by eruptions of the intense flooding power of unconscious. The greatest renowed psychologist, C. G. Jung, is believed to have been crazy. Jung was a divine visionary and extraordinary prophet of our age as zeitgeist,the Spirit of Time (C. G. Jung. 2009. *The Red Book.* Norton, edited by Sonu Shamdasani).

Divine Mad brings light to his culture by functioning as compensatory process to humanity and her lost soul. He is a repository of the ancient knowledge, keeper of the archaic and primordial Soul of our Ancestors that has been ripped apart by Religious Dogmas as well as by monistic scientific paradigms. The ancient Myth of the ancient civilizations who lived in the Anima Mundi has been turned off by the emerging Myth of the Science and of the technology.The Ancient soul that lives in anima mundi, the spirit of ancestors appears as chonic and residual activation of primal mind appearing in ordinary psychotic phenomena and borderline schizophrenic neuroses. These phenomena are "psychoid" in nature, because they are found at the threshold of consciousness, i.e., in a liminal zone.

The borderline individual is like a hero and Titan, struggling between the two worlds (between the superpersonal forces of the unconscious and, in-between the collective forces that tend to destroy him/her while he cannot work in the two worlds at the same time.

Dogmas have killed "God" and "Eros." Christianity has repressed sex in spite of the unidirectional and ethic consciousness that lead into rationality and *consensus gentium.* Metaphysic is dead!

The Church and its followers have killed Metahysics as well as mythology. Chtonic revivals of the primordial psyche appear in psychosis and psychic illness in today's collective psychoses. There is only one way to save humanity, and that is by his dissociation and its daimons that are threaten by humanity in its contemporary conflicts.

The way is returning back to the Ancient Soul, as well as re-discovering the mystery of the Primal Soul of our Ancestors, by travelling to primordial territories of the unconscious psyche where mythology actually resides. But Divine Crazy is the promethean impulse that can get access to gods—the only creative hero whose divine prophecy can warn humanity in time, and the only one who can bring a new symbolic archetype of meaning to humanity; the one who can help humankind release his present detachment from the unconscious.

Even if the Divine Crazy is alienated from people around him he archetypally represents a spiritually elected hero. The one who can redeem humankind from his psychic and spiritual dissociation.

# BIBLIOGRAPHY

Aurobindo. 1964. *On the Veda*. Pondicherry.

Avalon, A. Sir John Woodroffe. 2003 (reprint). *The Serpent Power: The Secrets of Tantric and Shaktic Yoga*. Dover Publications.

Assagioli, R. 1965. *Psychosyntesis: A Manual of Principles and Techniques*. Hobbs, Dorman.

Bentov, I. 1990. *Micromotion of the Body as a Factor in Development of the Nervous System*, in White J edition.

Bohm, D. *The Holographic Paradigm*. Boulder, CO: Shambhala.

———. 1987. *Unfolding Meaning*. London: Ark.

———. 1983. *Wholeness and the Implicate Order*. London: Ark.

Capra, F. 1982. *The Turning Point: Science, Society, and the Rising Culture*. Simon and Schuster, Bantam.

———. 1975. *The Tao of Physics*.

Combs, A. 2002. *The Radiance of Being: Understanding the Grand Integral Vision; Living the Integral Life* (2nd ed.). St Paul, MN: Paragon House.

Coomaraswamy, A.K. 1943. *Hinduism and Buddhism*. New York: Philosophical Library.

———. 1969. *The Dance of Shiva* New York: The Noonday Press.

Conze, E. 1958, 1975. *Buddhist Wisdom Books*. London: George Allen & Unwin.

Corbin, H.1969, 1998. *Creative Imagination in the Sufism of Ibn 'Arabi*. Princeton, N.J: Princeton University Press. Re-issued in 1998 as *Alone with the Alone*.

Danielou, A. 2002 "Mythes et dieux de l'Inde" Editions du Rocher.

Eliade, M. 1958. *Yoga, Immortality and Freedom*. translated by W. R. Trask. London: Routledge & Kegan Paul.

Ferrer, Jorge.2002. *Revisioning Transpersonal Theory*. Albany, N.Y: State University New York Press.

Filippani, Ronconi P. 1987. *Vak, La Parola Primordiale*. Messina: Ed. Pungitopo.

Gnoli, R. 1999. "Tantraloka di Abhinavagupta," in *Luce delle Sacre Scritture*. Milano: Adelphi Edizioni.

Teun Goudriaan and Sanjugupta. 1981. *Hindu Tantric and Sakta Literature*. Wiesbaden.

Chamberlain, D. B. 1981. Birth Recall in Hypnosis. *Birth Psychology Bulletin, 2*(2), 14-18.

———.1987. Consciousness at Birth: The Range of Empirical Evidence. In T. R. Verny (ed.), *Pre- and*

*Perinatal Psychology: An Introduction*. 69-90. New York: Human Sciences.

Greyson, B. 1985. A Typology of Near-Death Experiences. *American Journal of Psychiatry*, 142, 967-969.

————.1990. Near-Death Encounters With and Without Near-Death Experiences: Comparative NDE Scale Profiles. *Journal of Near-Death Studies*, 8(3), 151-161.

Grof, S. 1976. *Realms of Human Unconscious*. New York: Viking.

Grof, S. & C. Grof. 1980. *Beyond Death*. London: Thames and Hudson.

Grof, S. 1987. *The Adventure of Self Discovery*. State University of New York Press, Albany NY.

Grof, S. & C. Grof.1989. "Spiritual Emergency: When Personal Transformation becomes a Crisis" (*New Consciousness Reader*). Los Angeles: J. P. Tarcher.

Grof, S. 1975. *Realms of the Human Unconscious: Observations from LSD Research*. New York: Viking Press.

————. 1980. *LSD Psychotherapy*. Pomona, CA: Hunter House.

————. 1985. *Beyond the Brain: Birth, Death, and Transcendence in Psychotherapy*. Albany, N.Y: State University New York Press.

————. 1988. *The Adventure of Self-Discovery*. Albany, N.Y.: State University New York Press

Grof, S., H. Zina Bennett. 1992. *Holotropic Mind*. San Francisco: Harper Collins MAPS.

Grof, S. 1998. *The Cosmic Game: Exploration of the Frontiers of Human Consciousness* Albany, N.Y: State University New York Press.

———. 2006. *The Ultimate Journey: Consciousness and the Mystery of Death.* San Francisco: Harper Collins MAPS.

———. 2000. *Psychology of the Future.* Lesson from Modern Consciousness Research.

Grof, S. & C. Grof. 2000. *The Stormy Search of the Self.* New York: Perigee Books. Albany, N.Y: State University New York Press.

Grof, S. 2001. *LSD Psychotherapy.* Florida: MAPS.

———*Realms of the Human Unconscious: Observations from LSD Research*

Viking Press, New York, 1975. Paperback: E. P. Dutton, New York, 1976.

———*The Human Encounter with Death.*

E. P. Dutton, New York, 1977 (with Joan Halifax).

———*LSD Psychotherapy.*

Hunter House, Pomona, California, 1980.

———*Beyond Death: Gates of Consciousness.*

Thames & Hudson, London, 1980 (with Christina Grof).

———*Ancient Wisdom and Modern Science.*

State University New York (SUNY) Press, Albany, N.Y., 1984 (ed.).

———*Beyond the Brain: Birth, Death, and Transcendence in Psychotherapy.*

State University New York (SUNY) Press, Albany, N.Y., 1985.

———*The Adventure of Self-Discovery.*

State University New York (SUNY) Press, Albany, N.Y., 1987.

———*Human Survival and Consciousness Evolution.*

State University New York (SUNY) Press, Albany, N.Y., 1988 (ed.).

———*Spiritual Emergency: When Personal Transformation Becomes a Crisis.*

J. P. Tarcher, Los Angeles, 1989 (ed. with Christina Grof).

———*The Stormy Search for the Self: A Guide to Personal Growth Through Transformational Crises.* Los Angeles: J. P. Tarcher, Los Angeles, 1991 (with Christina Grof).

———*The Holotropic Mind: The Three Levels of Consciousness and How They Shape Our Lives.*

Harper Collins, San Francisco, CA (with Hal Zina Bennett), 1994.

———*Books of the Dead: Manuals for Living and Dying.*

Thames and Hudson, London, 1994.

———*The Cosmic Game: Exploration of the Frontiers of Human Consciousness.* State University New York (SUNY) Press, Albany, N.Y.,1998.

Jung, C. G. 1956. *Symbols of Transformation*. Collected Works, vol. 5, Bollingen Series XX, Princeton, N.J.: Princeton University Press.

———. 1959. *The Archetypes and the Collective Unconscious*. Collected Works, vol. 9,1. Bollingen Series XX, Princeton, N. J.: Princeton University Press.

———. 1960. *A Review of the Complex Theory*. Collected Works, vol. 8, Bollingen Series XX. Princeton: Princeton University Press.

———. 2009. Sonu Shamdasani, ed. *The Red Book*. Norton.

Neumann, Erich. 1972. *The Great Mother*. Princeton, N.J.: Princeton University Press.

Moody, R. A. & P. Perry. 1988. *The Light Beyond*. New York: Bantam.

Moody, R. A. 1975. *Life after Life*. Covington, GA: Mockingbird.

———. 1977. *Reflections on Life after Life*. San Francisco: Cameron.

Krippner, S. 1989. Some touchstones for parapsychological research. In G. K. Zollschan, J. F. Schumaker, & G. F. Walsh (eds.), *Exploring the paranormal: Perspectives on belief and experience* (167-183). Lindfield, New South Wales, Australia: Unity Press.

———. 1990. Frontiers in dreamwork. In S. Krippner (ed.), *Dreamtime and dreamwork: Decoding the language of the night* (207-213). Los Angeles: Tarcher.

————. 1993. Telepathy and dreaming. In M.A. Carskadon (ed.), *Encyclopedia of sleep and dreaming* (612-613). New York: Macmillan.

————. 1994. Waking life, dream life, and the construction of reality. *Anthropology of Consciousness*, 5(3), 17-24.

Krippner, S. & Welch, P. 1992. *Spiritual dimensions of healing: From native shamanism to contemporary health care.* New York: Irvington.

Krippner, S., & J. Dillard. 1988. *Dreamworking.* Buffalo, NY: Bearly.

Krippner, S., M. Ullman & M. Honorton. 1971. A precognitive dream study with a single subject. *Journal of the American Society for Psychical Research*, 65, 192-203.

Krippner, S. & A. Villoldo. 1986. *The realms of healing* (3rd ed.). Berkeley, CA: Celestial Arts

Krippner, S. 1989. Mythological aspects of death and dying. In A. Berger et al. (eds.), *Perspectives on death and dying* (3-13). Philadelphia: Charles Press.

————. 1990. Tribal shamans and their travels into dreamtime. In S. Krippner (ed.), *Dreamtime and dreamwork: Decoding the language of the night* (185-193). Los Angeles: Jeremy P. Tarcher/Perigee.

Krippner, S. & Faith, L. 2001. Exotic dreams: A cross-cultural study. *Dreaming, 11*, 73-82.

Laszlo, E. 1987. The psi-field hypothesis. *IS Journal, 4*, 13-28.

———. 1993. *The creative cosmos: A unified science of matter, life, and mind.* Edinburgh: Floris.

———. 1997. *The whispering pond.* New York: Harper Collins.

———. 2001, Sept. 1. Human evolution in the third millennium. *Futures,* 1-11.

———. 2004. *Science and the Akashic field: An integral theory of everything.* Rochester, NY: Inner Traditions.

Pribram, K. H. 1971. *Languages of the brain: Experimental paradoxes and principles in neuropsychology.* Englewood Cliffs, NJ: Prentice-Hall

———.1991. *Brain and perception: Holonomy and structure in figural processing.* Hillsdale, NJ: Lawrence Erlbaum Associates.

Ring K. 1980. *Life at death: Scientific investigation of the near-death experience.* New York: Coward, McCann & Geoghegan.

———. 1984. *Heading toward Omega: Insearch of the meaning of the near-death experience.* New York: William Morrow.

Ring, K. & M. Lawrence, M. 1993. Further evidence for veridical perception during near-death experiences. *Journal of Near-Death Studies, 11,* 223-230.

Talbot, M. 1991. *The Holographic Universe.*

———. 1988. *Beyond the Quantum.* New York: Bantam Books.

Wade, J. 1996. *Changes of mind: A holonomic theory of the evolution of consciousness.* Albany: State University of New York Press.

Wolf, Alan F. *The Dreaming Universe: Investigations of the Middle Realm of Consciousness and Matter* (New York: Summit Books, 1993).

Greyson, B. 1993. The Physio-kuṇḍalinī syndrome and mental illness. *Journal of Transpersonal Psychology*, 25,43,58, Psyc Info Abstract, Accession Number.

———. 2000. Some Neuropsychological correlates of the phisyo-kuṇḍalinī syndrome. *Journal of Transpersonal Psychology*, 32,123-134, PsycInfo Abstract.

Grof, S. *Realms of Human Unconscious*, New York: Viking, 1975.

Grof, S. & C. Grof. 1980. *Beyond Death*. London: Thames and Hudson.

Grof, S. 1988. *The Adventure of Self Discovery*. Albany, NY: State University of New York Press.

Grof, S. & C. Grof. 1989. *Spiritual Emergency: When Personal Transformation becomes a Crisis (New Consciousness Reader)*, Los Angeles, J.P. Tarcher.

Grof, S., H. Zina Bennett. 1992. *The Holotropic mind*. San Francisco: Harper Collins MAPS.

Grof, S. 1998. *The Cosmic Game: Exploration of the Frontiers of Human Consciousness*. Albany, NY: State University of New York Press.

Grof, S. 2006. *The Ultimate Journey: Consciousness and the Mystery of Death*. MAPS.

———. 2000. *Psychology of the Future. Lesson from modern consciousness research*. Albany, NY: State University of New York Press.

Grof, S. & Grof C. 2000. *The Stormy Search for the Self.* New York Perigee/Tarcher Los Angeles, CA. Putnam Publications.

Hansen, G. 1995. Schizophrenia or Spiritual Crisis? "On Raising the Kuṇḍalinī" and its diagnostic classification, *Weekly Journal of Danish Medical Association.*

Hillman, J. 1985. *Anima, an anatomy of personified notion.* Princeton, N.J.: Princeton University Press & London: Routledge and Kegan Paul LTD.

Hillman, J. 1964, 1967. *Betrayal: Senex and Puer.*

James W. 1902. (first ed.), *The varieties of religious experience: A study in human nature.* New York: The modern library, Original edition 1902. New York and London: Longmans Green and Company.

Jung, C. G. *Collected Works.* Princeton, N.J.: University Press and London: Routledge and Kegan Paul LTD.

———. 1960. *A Review of the Complex Theory.* Collected Works, vol. 8, Bollingen Series XX. Princeton: Princeton University Press.

Jung, C. G. and C. Kerényi. *Essays on a Science of Mythology.* Bollingen Series XXII New York: Pantheon Books, Inc. .

Jung C. G. 1969. *Mandala Symbolism.* R.F.C. Hull (transl.) vol. 9, Part I, Bollingen Series XX. Princeton, N.J.: Princeton University Press.

Krippner, S. 1989. Some touchstones for parapsychological research. In G. K. Zollschan, J. F. Schumaker, & G.F. Walsh (eds.), *Exploring the paranormal: Perspectives on belief and experience* (pp. 167-183). Lindfield, New South Wales, Australia: Unity Press.

———. 1990. Frontiers in dreamwork. In S. Krippner (ed.), *Dreamtime and dreamwork: Decoding the language of the night* (pp. 207-213). Los Angeles: Tarcher.

———. 1993. Telepathy and dreaming. In M. A. Carskadon (ed.), *Encyclopedia of sleep and dreaming* (pp. 612-613). New York: Macmillan.

———. 1994. Waking life, dream life, and the construction of reality. *Anthropology of Consciousness,5*(3), 17-24.

Krippner, S. & Dillard, J. 1988. *Dreamworking*. Buffalo, NY: Bearly.

Krippner, S., Ullman, M., & Honorton, M. 1971. A precognitive dream study with a single subject. *Journal of the American Society for Psychical Research, 65*, 192-203.

Krippner, S. & Vitoldo, A. 1986. *The realms of healing* (3rd ed.). Berkeley, CA: Celestial Arts

Krippner, S., & Welch, P. 1992. *Spiritual dimensions of healing: From native shamanism to contemporary health care*. New York: Irvington.

Krishnamurti, J. 1954. The First and Last Freedom, Krishnamurti Writings, Inc., Ojay USA.

————. 1969. *Freedom from the Known*. London: Victor Gollancz, Ltd. .Krishnamurti Foundation London.

————. 1995. On Truth. San Francisco: Harper. Krishnamurti Foundation Trust Ltd London.

*Krishnamurti's Notebook*, 1976, Krishnamurti Publications of America expanded 2004 edition. Published journal that Krishnamurti kept between June 1961 and March 1962.

*Krishnamurti's Journal*, 1982, Harper & Row 1982. A personal journal that was started in 1973 and kept intermittently until 1975.

*Krishnamurti to Himself: His Last Journal*, 1987, HarperCollins 1993 paperback. Transcribed from audio tape recordings made at his home in the Ojai Valley between February 1983 and March 1984.

Lukoff, David, Lu, Francis G., Turner, R. 1998. *From Spiritual Emergency to Spiritual Problem: the Transpersonal roots of the New D-S-M-IV Category*, Journal of Humanistic Psychology, 38 (2),21-50.

Maslow, A. 1962-68. *Toward a Psychology of Being*. London and New York: Van Nostranand Reinhold Co.

Miller, J. 1972. *The Vedas "Harmony, Meditation and Fulfilment,"* Rider and Company London 1974.

Neumann, E. 1970. *Origins and History of Consciousness*. Princeton, N.J.: Princeton University Press.

———. 1972. *The Great Mother*. Princeton, N.J.: Princeton University Press.

Pribram, K. H. 1970. "Feelings as monitors." In M. B. Arnold *Feelings and Emotions*. New York: Academic Press.

Sannella, Lee. 1975. *Kundalini, psychosis or transcendence?* San Francisco: Dakin.

Scotton, Bruce, and Battista (eds.). 1996. *The phenomenology and treatment of kuṇḍalinī*, in "Chinen, Textbook of

Transpersonal Psychiatry and Psychology." New York: Basic Books Inc. PsycInfo Abstract.

Singh, J., Lakshmanjee J. 1988. *Abhinavagupta, Parātrīśikā vivarana, the Secret of Tantric Mysticism*, Sri Jainendra press, Motilal Banarsidass, Delhi.

Talbot M. 1991. *The Holographic Universe.*

———. 1998. *Beyond the quantum*. New York: Bantam.

Tarnas, R. 2006. *Cosmos and Psyche: Intimations of a New World View*. Viking Penguin.

Tarnas R., *The Passion of the Western mind:understanding the idea that have shaped our world view*. New York Ballantine Books.

G.Tucci, *Induismo*, "Hinduism." ISMEO Roma.

Von Glasenapp, H. 1949. Philosophie der Inder. Alfred Verlag Stuttgart.

Watts, A.W. 1966. *The Book: On the Taboo Against Knowing Who You Are*. New York: Pantheon.

———. 1975. *Tao: The Watercourse Way*. New York: Pantheon.

———. 1983. *Way of Liberation*. ed. Mark Watts. New York: Weatherhill.

———. *Talking Zen*. New York and Tokyo: Weatherhill.

———. 1957. *The Way of Zen*. Pantheon.

White, J. 1990. *Kuṇḍalinī Evolution and Enlightenment*. Paragon House: New York.

Wilber, K. 1977. *The Spectrum of Consciousness*. Wheaton, Ill.: Quest.

———. 1981. *Up from Eden*. New York: Doubleday/ Anchor.

———. 1982. *A Social God*. New York McGraw-Hill.

Wilber K. *The Atman project: A transpersonal view of human development*. Wheaton, Ill.: The Theosophical Publishing House 1980.

———. 1982. *The Holographic Paradigm and Other Paradoxes*. Boston: Shambhala, Boston.

Wilber, K., Engler, J., Brown, D.P. 1986. *Transformation of Consciousness: conventional and contemplative perspectives on development*. Boston and London: Shambhala.

———. 2000. *A Brief History of Everything*. Shambhala.

———. 2000. *Integral Psychology*. Shambhala.

Williams, Paul, with Anthony Tribe. 2000. *Buddhist Thought: A Complete Introduction to the Indian Tradition*. London.

Wolf, Alan F. 1993. *The Dreaming Universe: Investigations of the Middle Realm of Consciousness and Matter*. Summit Books: New York.

———. The Quantum Pshysics of Consciousness: Towards a New Psychology, "Integrative Psychology," Vol. 3 (1985), pp. 236-47; On the Quantum Physical Theory of Subjective Antedating, "Journal of Theoretical Biology," Vol. 136 (1989), 13-19.

————. 1981. *Taking the Quantum Leap: The New Physics for Nonscientists*, ed. riv. San Francisco: Harper & Row.

Zimmer, H., edited by Campbell J. 1946. *Myths and Symbols in Indian Art and Civilization.* Bollingen Foundation Washington D.C., Princeton University Press, Princeton, N.J.

Pignatelli D., Il Risveglio dell'Intelligenza:Verso una nuova Psicologia dell'Essere (Montedit 2007,Uni Service 2008,& MyBook 2010).

- Revisioned in the Journal of Transpersonal Psychology JTP Vol 40 n 1 2008 and signaled in the JTP Vol 41 n 1.

- Psiche Primordiale:il misterioso richiamo dell'Anima degli Antenati- (Primordial Psyche) US translation upcoming.

# INDEX

**D**